CLEVER MAN
THE LIFE OF PADDY COMPASS NAMADBARA

AS TOLD BY:
BIG BILL NEIDJIE, BLUEY ILKGIRR, JACOB NAYINGGUL,
JIM WAUCHOPE, JOHNNY WILLIAMS SNR, RON COOPER,
THOMPSON YULUDJIRI AND OTHERS
COMPILED BY IAN WHITE

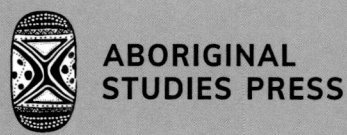

ABORIGINAL
STUDIES PRESS

Published in 2020
by Aboriginal Studies Press
Reprinted 2021

© Ian White in compilation, 2020
© Individual stories held by individual storytellers, 2020
© 'The Perfection of the Morning', Sharon Butala, 2005. With permission of the author.

Big Bill Neidjie, Bluey Ilkgirr, Jacob Nayinggul, Jim Wauchope, Johnny Williams Snr, Ron Cooper, Thompson Yuludjiri, Jamesie Wauchope, Susan Ngaladjingu Ilkgirr, Robert Djorlom, Ningoldie 'Goldie' Blyth, Alan Randall, Shorty Dirdi and Nelson Mulurinj

All rights reserved. No part of this book may be reproduced or transmitted in any form or by any means, electronic or mechanical, including photocopying, recording or by any information storage and retrieval system, without prior permission in writing from the publisher. The *Australian Copyright Act 1968* (the Act) allows a maximum of one chapter or 10 per cent of this book, whichever is the greater, to be photocopied by any educational institution for its education purposes provided that the educational institution (or body that administers it) has given a remuneration notice to Copyright Agency Limited (CAL) under the Act.

The opinions expressed in this book are the authors' own and do not necessarily reflect the view of AIATSIS or ASP.

Aboriginal and Torres Strait Islander people are respectfully advised that this publication contains names and images of deceased persons, and culturally sensitive information.

Aboriginal Studies Press is the publishing arm of the Australian Institute of Aboriginal and Torres Strait Islander Studies.

GPO Box 553, Canberra, ACT 2601
Phone: 02 6246 1183
Fax: 02 6261 4288
Email: asp@aiatsis.gov.au
Web: www.aiatsis.gov.au/asp/about.html

 A catalogue record for this book is available from the National Library of Australia

ISBN: 9781925302233 (pb)
       9781925302240 (ePub)
       9781925302264 (ebook PDF)

Cover image: 'Maam, malignant spirit', c. 1963 by Paddy Namadbara. Image supplied by National Gallery of Australia
Designed by Christine Bruderlin
Printed by SOS Print + Media, Sydney

'Ian White's book offers a unique historical glimpse into an Aboriginal world on the cusp of change due to European incursion; it reveals an authentic insight into the special relationship of the 'clever man' with his Dreaming spirits and his process of initiation into the special knowledge of a marrkidjbu. White compiled his generalised account of 'Old Paddy', aka Paddy Compass Namadbara, from a number of Western Arnhem Land people for whom Old Paddy had been a major figure in their lives. Recording various accounts, White's extraordinary work shows Old Paddy's special talent for healing the sick, exercising wisdom, and having visions in which he foresaw future events, for which he offered guidance and strategies for dealing with Western encroachment. Old Paddy's visions of the future foretold major events that were astonishing in the 1950s: Aboriginal people would get paid for their work, would own land and cars, and that money issues would bring division. All of his predictions came true. A rare insight into the world of the Dreaming, this book is unique and essential reading.'

Susan Greenwood, University of Sussex

'Forty years since the passing of Paddy Compass Namadbara, his legacy still looms large amongst the people of Western Arnhem Land. Ian White has dedicated decades to recording the story of Namadbara's life and here he presents an extraordinary biography as told by the people of this region of the Northern Territory. The anecdotes about Namadbara's exceptional powers as a 'clever man' portray him as a community leader, teacher, sage, mystic, counsellor and healer. These are however more than just marvellous stories that defy explanation and evoke our wonder. The events of Namadbara's life, described by so many witnesses from both sides of the cultural divide, and collated so respectfully in this book, are an ongoing challenge to how various fields of the social and cognitive sciences should deal with such matters.'

Dr Murray Garde OAM, ANU

'This powerful and sensitive portrait of Paddy Compass Namadbara, a Western Arnhem Land marrkidjbu, or clever man, deserves a place among the classic works on shamanism. Told principally through the words of those who knew Namadbara and benefitted from his power, the book provides a rich and thought-provoking account of his extraordinary life and works. White, an anthropologist with decades of experience in the region, provides just enough commentary to help orient readers to the social and historical context, while allowing the knowledge and stories of Western Arnhem Landers themselves to take center stage. It is a masterful book that will be of interest to indigenous people everywhere as well as to scholars in anthropology and indigenous studies.'

Paul Nadasdy, Professor of Anthropology and American Indian and Indigenous Studies at Cornell University

'Clever Man is a wonderfully rich, complex and sometimes mysterious biography, founded in Aboriginal men's memories of a healer of the highest degree, who died in the Kakadu region in 1978. Paddy Compass diagnosed illness by x-ray vision, brought willy willys into existence and dead animals back to life. He foresaw the future, provided confident assurance in turbulent times, and gave men purpose. Ian White leaves the memories to speak for themselves but in his afterword sympathetically examines how the paranormal phenomena and the insights into a non-western consciousness might be understood. This is a deeply empathetic record, opening up a rare glimpse into another world.'

Emeritus Professor Nicholas Peterson, ANU

Namadbara at his beach camp, Mountnorris Bay, 1973. Photo: George Chaloupka.

Contents

Preface	vii
The tellers of the story — the main accounts	xiii
A note on the rendering of Aboriginal English	xviii
Introduction	1
Making of a Clever Man — Acquiring the Power	8
The sugarbag event	8
Speaking with the yumbarrbarr	12
The Power of the Marrkidjbu	16
Kumula: Giving purpose for that job	16
Healing — defeating namorrorddo	18
Removing 'sickness objects'	22
Healing himself	25
Healing — Balanda accounts	25
Sorcery	27
Manifestations of Power	29
Water divining	29
Namadbara and nature	30
Clever knowledge	31
The world of the dead	33
Namadbara's reputation	38
Kumula and the Wider Community	40
Dreams and visions	40
'Marrkidjbu — but stronger and something else'	42
Making leaders for the community	45
Controlling the power of Ngalyod, the Rainbow Serpent	48
Passing on the Power	53
Namadbara's 'power objects'	53
'He gave me this gift'	55
'This power, too hard'	57
His Death — and After	66
Namadbara's post-death influence	67
Namadbara's Legacy	71
Afterword	75
Acknowledgements	87
Paddy Compass Namadbara: A Putative Timeline	89
Glossary	91
Endnotes	95
Bibliography	100

List of Illustrations

Namadbara at his beach camp, Mountnorris Bay, 1973 ii
Wurrakak (Tor Rock), a significant site on the southeastern
bounds of Namadbara's Country viii
Lanka (Mt Permain), a major regional and spiritually
dangerous sacred area, central to Namadbara's Alarrdju estate xi
'Two Mimi Spirits (males) dancing' by Paddy Compass Namadbara,
Croker Island, 1963 2
'Two Mimi Spirits (males) dancing' by Paddy Compass Namadbara,
Croker Island, 1963 5
'Maam, malignant spirit', c. 1963, by Paddy Namadbara 6
'Maam, malignant spirit', c. 1963, by Paddy Namadbara 9
Bark painting 'Namorrordo, malicious spirit of the Stone Country'
by Charlie Najombolmi, Balawurru 21
Views of the extensive main billabong at Mangulwan where
Namadbara's spirit is said to reside 35
Namadbara (third from left), in his role as leader and overseeing
guide for an 'expedition' to Mt Borradaile, in the context of
establishing the First Aboriginal Mining Company (FAMCO), 1971. 46
On a visit to Namadbara's country in 2003, his nephew Archie Brown
performs mortuary ritual ochreing at Namadbara's old camp site at
Mangulwan where his spirit resides. Photo: Murray Garde 59
Namadbara's nephew Archie Brown, linguist Nicholas Evans
and archaeologist Kim Akerman pay their respects at
Namadbara's grave, Mountnorris Bay, 2003 63
Director of the Australian Institute of Aboriginal Studies (now AIATSIS),
Professor Neil W. G. Macintosh, under the guidance and strict
instructions from Namadbara, is conducted to the major sacred site
complex of Awunbarna (Mt Borradaile) in 1971. 69
Gunbalanya/Oenpelli community from Injalak Hill 74

Map
Locations and area mentioned in the text. xx

Preface

I first heard of Paddy Compass in 1988 when I was working in the Murgenella region of northwestern Arnhem Land, employed as an anthropologist with the Northern Land Council (NLC). At the time 'buffalo royalty' money — from a government sponsored campaign to eradicate brucellosis and tuberculosis from the wild buffalo population — was being paid to the members of clan groups who had 'Country' (i.e. traditional clan estates) in the buffalo culling zones. My task was to consult with members of each clan group and establish a list of those recognised as rightful members of the group for the purpose of receiving a share of the money. One clan was especially problematic in terms of this exercise. There were three lineages, two relating most strongly to one half of the clan's estate and the third to the other half. The members of one lineage had long lived in Darwin and insisted that both matrifiliates and patrifiliates should be eligible. The members of the other two lineages who lived on or close to their clan land considered that the clan had to abide by the traditional way in its method of recruitment and recognition, they presented a strict patrilineal interpretation of land ownership, the differences leading to a long and quite bitter dispute within the clan. The question of membership had not been a big issue until then, but, with the question of access to royalties hanging in the balance, it suddenly was. One of the residents at Murgenella, Jim Wauchope, an Aboriginal man originally from Central Australia who had lived and worked in the area for over forty years and well knew the local people and their life-histories, was offering some advice and comment. Jim was dismayed to see such serious arguments arising within the clan group itself. It was a development he had not seen before, brother against brother, arguing over money. He was particularly dismayed that the first time large sums of money were coming into the area this should happen. He felt a foreboding about the future

Wurrakak (Tor Rock), a significant site on the southeastern bounds of Namadbara's Country. Photo: Murray Garde.

and feared this was the fourth event 'Old Paddy' had predicted. I didn't know who 'Old Paddy' was, nor anything about his predictions. I was curious. Jim began:

> It must have been back in the 50s, long before Aboriginal people had any of the rights that they have today, that that Old Man had had a vision. He had foreseen four major events that would come to affect Aboriginal people. He told me the first thing he saw in his vision was Aboriginal people getting paid money for their work 'just like white fellas'. The second was that Aboriginal people would come to own their land — that they would be bosses for their land, like white fellas — that they'd have rights to the land. The third was of Aboriginal people owning motor cars, getting around in motor cars. Just like white fellas.

Jim said that to hear something like that back in the 1950s, considering the status of Aboriginal people at that time, was astonishing. But when, in the later 1960s, he 'lived to see' equal wages being paid to Aboriginal people for work on cattle stations, he began to think that Paddy's prediction had been accurate. And then he saw the second of Paddy's predictions realised with the winning of land rights under the *Aboriginal Land Rights (Northern Territory) Act 1976*. Soon afterwards, with royalties coming from mining ventures on Aboriginal land, it became a common sight to see Aboriginal people driving around in their own Toyotas. He had lived, he said, to see three of Paddy's predictions come true, one by one. Now it seemed that the fourth prediction was coming true, despite his hope that it was wrong: that money issues would result in serious fighting within the clan itself — establishing bitter family divisions and threatening the cohesiveness and the traditional clan structure of the very group.

I was fascinated by this account. Jim didn't tell me much more about Paddy other than that they had worked together for years in the bush, buffalo and crocodile shooting, and timber work. Jim clearly had great respect for him and implied the old man was gifted, that he was 'clever'. He mentioned that he had been healed by Paddy on occasions when he was sick. He said I should go and speak to another old man at Cannon Hill if I wanted to know more about him, which is what I did . . . I was hooked.

And some weeks later I introduced myself to this old man, Big Bill Neidjie, a prominent spokesperson and an eminent storyteller of the region. Having spent an hour or so with old man Bill at Cannon Hill, recording some of his stories about 'Old Compass', I was driving back out of the outstation (small Aboriginal homeland community) in the northeast of Kakadu National Park, when a man visiting from the nearby Aboriginal township of Gunbalanya called out to me, asking what I'd been doing talking to the old man. When I told him, he responded immediately, saying that I must go and ask 'Jacob' at Gunbalanya to tell me 'about the cat'. And so it went on from there.

Many others have told me of their own special experiences with Namadbara. Some volunteered their reminiscences and several told stories of how he had powerfully and positively affected their lives. It was clear from these accounts that Namadbara was widely considered to have been both a wise man, in that people looked to him for advice, and a very powerful man, in terms of both the mundane and 'otherworldly' powers. Through the exercise of these powers or abilities, he had the reputation of being, as he was described to me, a 'properly number one marrkidjbu' (a powerful clever man of the highest rank). In the opinion of those who told his stories, he was considered the last of such men in Western Arnhem Land; the last of those who were able to achieve such a high status and outstanding reputation.

'Clever' is a term used in many Aboriginal communities to refer to a person with special powers, often used for healing. Besides being a local Aboriginal English term for psychic or magic practices, I use this term by preference throughout the story as I believe it captures the dignity and respect of the practice generally accorded it by the people. A clever man or, less frequently, clever woman, exhibits powers and abilities beyond ordinary humans and is generally held in high esteem by their community. As Namadbara's story is told, the source and extent of these powers will become evident.

The area over which Namadbara's reputation extended is the western part of Western Arnhem Land, principally the communities of Gunbalanya (Oenpelli), Minjilang (Croker Island), Cobourg Peninsula and Warruwi (Goulburn Island), where the languages of Kunwinjku, Iwaidja and Maung are largely spoken.

The portrait of Paddy Compass Namadbara presented here has been constructed from the accounts given by a number of Western Arnhem Landers who have each recalled aspects of Namadbara's life, particularly those aspects that impinged the most significantly on their lives. Each of these were countrymen of Namadbara and had either lived and worked closely with him, or had spent time within the circle of his family group. As such, the portrait is based on their memories and reconstructions of conversations that they had with him. The portrait has, however, been put together by someone who never met the man and is not a member of his culture — a Balanda (non-Aboriginal). So necessarily it has the limitations that the process of recall, memory, reconstruction and cross-cultural perspectives are subject to. The attempt is to present, as much as possible, the portrait in the words of Namadbara's fellow Western Arnhem Landers, to let the accounts speak for themselves. This inevitably involves some stitching together of accounts in the effort to present coherence. However, a life does have a logic that grows out of the fact that it has been lived with other people. And I have sought to find that logic of progression. In attempting this, I may end up somewhat distorting the

Lanka (Mt Permain), a major regional and spiritually dangerous sacred area, central to Namadbara's Alarrdju estate. In his book *Lamilami speaks*, regional elder Lazarus Lamilami writes (1974:26): 'On the mainland, going west from Goulburn Island and inland into Yiwadja [Iwaidja] Country, the most important place is Langa. It is djang and it is ngunjug, sacred. Only one man is allowed to go there, and that is Paddy Compass . . . Langa is a very special place and no one else is allowed to go there at all. Not even Paddy's sons.' Photo: Murray Garde.

'truth' of his life, of not corresponding with the view of any particular one of his fellow Western Arnhem Landers. If so, I would hope that any distortion is not too great. Western Arnhem Landers may judge this for themselves.

The tellers of the story —
the main accounts

'Big Bill' Neidjie, nakamarrang subsection, Bunidj clan

Bill was born on the East Alligator River in the neighbourhood of his father's Bunidj clan land — land that is now part of Kakadu National Park. As a teenager, after his father died, he moved with his mother into her Country on Cooper Creek and in closer contact with Namadbara. He spent his working life on the Arnhem Land coastal trading luggers and in the northwest Arnhem buffalo, crocodile and timber mill industry work camps alongside Namadbara who, some fifteen years his senior, became a significant mentor for Bill. In his later years, after the establishment of the *Aboriginal Land Rights (Northern Territory) Act 1976*, Bill became a prominent spokesperson, along with three other regional elders, in Aboriginal land-management affairs dealing with Kakadu National Park and Northern Land Council issues. He was often sought out by visiting non-Aboriginals as a regional 'culture spokesperson' (e.g. Neidjie et al. 1986; Neidjie 1989). Bill was awarded an OAM in 1989 for service to conservation. He died in 2002.

Bluey Ilkgirr

Bluey Ilkgirr, nabulanj subsection, Ildukidj clan

Born in the 1920s, nabulanj Bluey, after his early years on Oenpelli mission (Gunbalanya), moved around the region like many of the men of this era, seeking work in return for basic subsistence living supplies. At times he was a horseman on cattle stations, worked in the buffalo and crocodile skinning work camps, and at the Mudginberri meatworks. He returned frequently to Oenpelli. In this way, he was in frequent interaction with Namadbara as a regionally renowned healer. He considers that he was spiritually 'grown up' by Namadbara. In his later years, Bluey was a much in demand artist residing in Kakadu National Park. Bluey has passed away.

Jacob Nayinggul

Jacob Nayinggul, nakodjok subsection, Manilakarr clan

As nakodjok Jacob tells it, he was born and grew up 'in the bush' in his father's traditional Country to the south and west of Gunbalanya, and did not come in to the Gunbalanya mission community until his father died when Jacob was a teenager in the mid-1950s. He was then 'taken under Namadbara's wing' for some months and through his assistance, was propelled rapidly through the local school education system and soon into community leadership roles. He was not only the eminent Manilakarr clan leader but, even as a relatively young man — being a very eloquent spokesperson — he became a prominent elder within the whole community at Gunbalanya and active as a decision-maker in the wider Kakadu National Park issues. He died in 2012 and was buried on his Country in Mikkinj valley.

Jim Wauchope, nakangila subsection, Yulukidj clan

Jim was born in Central Australia but as a youngster, was taken to Minjilang (Croker Island), which had become a very strict centre for Stolen Generation children. He eventually married and raised a family and spent the rest of his life in this northwest region of Arnhem Land, often in close contact with Namadbara in the various work camps on the mainland as well as in the Minjilang community. For Jim, Namadbara was a major teacher. Jim died in 2015.

Jim Wauchope

Johnny Williams Snr, nakamarrang subsection, Kamulkban clan

John was born on his mother's Country at Udawur, Reef Point, Cobourg Peninsula. As a child, he would travel with his mother, step-father and siblings by canoe between Cobourg Peninsula and Mudjeegarrdart (Kamulkban Country). He was a countryman of Namadbara's; his Country was immediately adjacent to Namadbara's. As John himself tells, as a young man, his life was radically altered via Namadbara's strategic assistance, which ultimately gained him a permanent job within the Public Works Department in Darwin. There he married a Larrakia woman and together they raised a family. On retirement from the Public Works, he divided his time between Darwin (his wife's Country) and his obligations as a clan leader on his Mudjeegarrdart Country in Western Arnhem Land. He passed away in 2006.

Johnny Williams Snr

Ron Cooper, Murran clan

Ron (Mulurinj), born in the mid-1920s, was the grandson of the larger-than-life adventurer and entrepreneur, Joe Cooper, and the only son of Rueben Cooper and his Thursday Island wife, Sally Koosney Ah Mat (see Whimpress & Cooper 2018). Ron grew up on Country (northwestern Arnhem Land) around his father's timber mill camps in the Cobourg Peninsula and Mountnorris Bay area, and was thus in close contact with Namadbara right throughout his early life. As Ron himself tells, during this time, he went 'right through the rules' [all the ceremonial initiations] under Namadbara's guidance. After the Second World War, he went to Darwin where he married and raised his children, and worked for many years as a quantity surveyor. However, throughout those years, he kept contact with Namadbara and the northwest Arnhem countrymen right up until Namadbara's death. Ron considered Namadbara to be his most significant teacher. He traces his Murran clan connection to Country partly through Namadbara's overall leadership, but more particularly through that of another influential leader, Arramunika, who called Ron 'son'. Ron died in 2002.

Thompson Yuludjiri

Thompson Yuludjiri, nakodjok subsection, Djalama clan

Nakodjok Thompson did not speak much of his own early childhood other than that he had spent much of it on Goulburn Island. Although born of a Djalama clansman whose Country is on the middle reaches of the Goomadeer River, in his paintings, Thompson said he followed the themes and stories of Namadbara's Country rather than those of Djalama, as he had been taken as a son into the family unit of Namadbara and his ngalkangila wife, Rhoda. He thus spent many years with Namadbara. In his later life, from its inception in the 1980s, he consistently worked at the Injalak Arts and Craft Centre at Gunbalanya, mentoring the younger painters and painting traditional themes and stories he had received from Namadbara. Thompson was also the main 'storyman' for the much acclaimed Australian theatrical productions 'Mimi' and 'Crying Baby'. He passed away in 2009.

Other storytellers:

Jamesie Wauchope (eldest son of Jim Wauchope)
Susan Ngaladjingu Ilkgirr
Robert Djorlom
Ningoldie 'Goldie' Blyth
Alan Randall
Shorty Dirdi
Nelson Mulurinj

The majority of interviews from which Namadbara's biography is reconstructed were conducted in 1995. The principal storytellers have all passed away. The families of each of the storytellers have given their permission to use their deceased ones' names and photographs. The majority of accounts were at least partially tape-recorded in addition to written notes being made. Copies of these cassette tapes and notes are held — under appropriate restrictions — within the Australian Institute of Aboriginal and Torres Strait Islander Studies (AIATSIS) in Canberra.

A note on the rendering of Aboriginal English

The conversations with the different storytellers were conducted in English, an English that ranged from Aboriginal English — including some Kriol phrases and a smattering of Kunwinjku — to Standard Australian English. Occasionally that variation even occurred within the one speech utterance. This has presented a difficulty in rendering this variable speech into written text. Unlike North Australian Kriol — the *lingua franca* of Aboriginal speakers in the Katherine, Barunga and Ngukurr areas — there are no established linguistic conventions for rendering north Australian Aboriginal English speech onto the written page. A further difficulty is in conveying meaning that is inherent in the spoken presentation. Although the words used are often sparse, so much meaning in the spoken text is given simply by a change in tone, a pause, or emphasis of a word. Such spoken features cannot easily be conveyed in text. Unfortunately, my level of Kunwinjku — its range of dialects now known by linguists as Bininj Kunwok (Garde 2013; Garde 2020) — was not sufficient to conduct conversations totally in Kunwinjku, nor in Iwaidja, the other prominent Western Arnhem language.

The use of 'bin' as a past tense marker on the verb that follows is used frequently in the texts. In addition, 'im' or 'em' are a regular feature of this Aboriginal English. Sometimes this stem is a suffix on a past tense phrase, as in, 'He bin killim you close' [He/It nearly killed you]. At others times, 'im' as a separate word may be a pronoun: 'he', 'she', 'him', 'her' or 'it', and 'em' may be 'them' or indeed 'he', 'she', 'it', 'him' or 'her'. The sense mostly comes out in the context, but it is not exact. This exercise is one of rendering the speech in an understandable fashion for the non-specialist reader, and still maintaining the feel of the original (see

Neidjie 1989 or Neidjie et al. 1986 for different presentations of Western Arnhem Aboriginal English).

I have tried to keep my translations into standard English to a minimum and only resorted to doing so when the meaning of the Aboriginal English text is insufficiently clear for the reader who is unfamiliar with this style of speech. This is partly that I would like the text — the words used in the account — to stand alone as much as possible, particularly as in one or two incidents related by the storytellers I myself am not clear as to what is 'really' going on (particularly the incident described on pages 48–51), and presenting a possible interpretation may mislead other readers rather than allowing them to come uncluttered to their own conclusions. In compiling this account of Namadbara's life, I am trying to tell the story for the benefit of future Western Arnhem Landers and thus to be as faithful as I can to the stories presented to me and not wrap them too much in the perspective of a Western observer writing for academic purposes. Although indeed, at the same time, I do want the text to serve that second purpose — with an academic readership in mind. To this latter purpose I have used endnotes and references extensively.

I have used the term 'Western Arnhem Landers' throughout rather than refer to specific language groups, as the stories of Paddy Compass Namadbara transcend linguistic boundaries — Kunwinjku, Iwaidja, Marrgu, Maung, Amurdak. Generally I have spelled place names using the Kunwinjku orthography with which I am familiar — whether the sites are located in Iwaidja or Kunwinjku Country — as until recently there has been no generally accepted Iwaidja orthography. However, the linguist Bruce Birch has now developed an Iwaidja orthography, and so for several clearly Iwaidja language sites, I have taken Bruce's advice and changed the spelling to accord with this orthography.

The English term 'clan' has now commonly been adopted by Western Arnhem Landers to refer to the named patrilineal land-owning groups known in Kunwinjku as kunmokurrkurr and in Iwaidja as namanamadj. Each clan thus has its own recognised named territory or 'estate' (see Berndt & Berndt 1970:54).

Note that it is the usual practice to refer to individuals by their 'skin' or sub-section name rather than their given name. So for instance, Namadbara is often referred to as 'Nabulanj', and his wife as 'Ngalkangila', rather than her Mission name, Rhoda.

Locations and area mentioned in the text

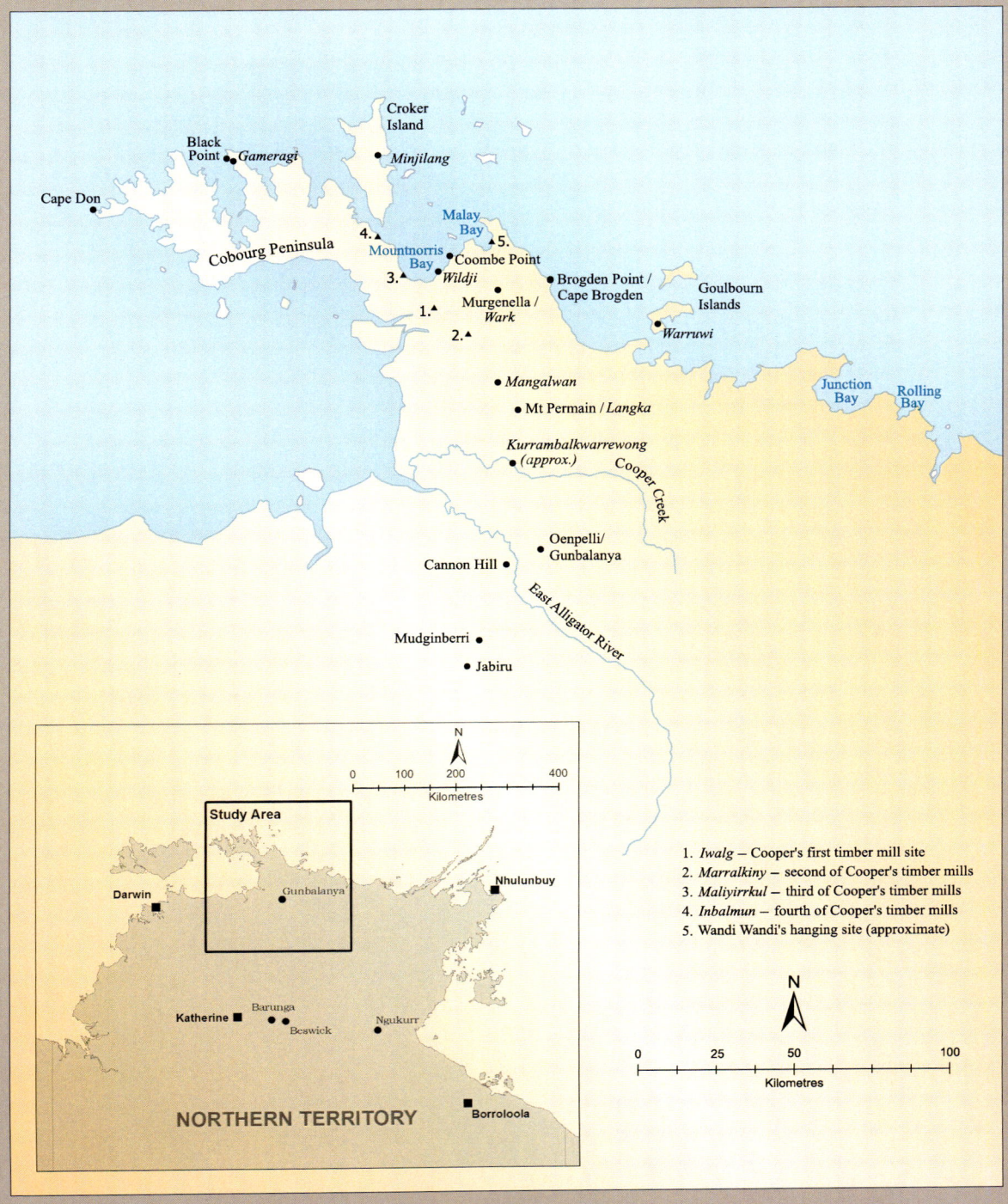

Introduction

Namadbara was born in northwestern Arnhem Land late in the nineteenth century (possibly 1898) on Cooper Creek, Country that is traditionally considered to belong to Amurdak speakers. Through his father and father's father, he inherited his identity as a member of the Alarrdju clan[1] whose land is within the neighbouring Iwaidja speaking territory. His mother belonged to the Murran clan whose land is also a part of Iwaidja territory. As an adult he was multilingual, like many of his fellows, not only speaking Iwaidja but also Kunwinjku (two major languages of the region) as well as English and no doubt Amurdak and possibly other now extinct or disappearing languages of the Cobourg–Croker Island region.

He died in 1978. During his life, he acquired and maintained the reputation among Western Arnhem Landers of being one of the most powerful and clever of traditional doctors, or marrkidjbu. The term marrkidjbu describes a person who has the special power (marrngkidj) to heal or, equally, to harm another. By the time of his passing, he was considered by many to have been the last of the truly powerful marrkidjbu. Those who spoke about him could point to no other marrkidjbu in this western region of Western Arnhem Land of such great stature and power as he.

In the eyes of his fellow Western Arnhem Landers, Namadbara achieved such a status through a combination of demonstrated clever abilities, including his success in healing the sick, his exercise of wisdom and his visions in which he foresaw future events. It was through those visions that he was able to offer guidance and strategies by which his countrymen might best deal with the constantly increasing encroachment of Western values, culture and technology into Western Arnhem Land.

'Two Mimi Spirits (males) dancing' by Paddy Compass Namadbara, Croker Island, 1963. Image supplied by NMA.

People looked to him, then, for leadership in the difficult times that his life spanned, leadership in coping with and, somehow, accommodating the presence among them of a foreign, powerful and dominating ideology. Christian missions had been established at Oenpelli (Gunbalanya) in 1925 by the Anglican Church Missionary Society (CMS) and, even earlier (1916), at Goulburn Island (Warruwi) by the Methodist Overseas Mission (Cole 1979; Lamilami 1974). Western adventurers and traders had begun roaming the Arnhem coastline bringing both threats and new opportunities and ways of life for Western Arnhem Landers (Hill 1951; Chaloupka et al. 1985).

The 1892 Cape Brogden massacre, where the crew of an Indonesian prau were killed by a party of northwestern Arnhem Landers led by Wandi Wandi (see Lamilami 1974:73; Searcy 1984:211–217), had occurred not long before Namadbara's birth. Wandi Wandi, the father of Namadbara's close brother Wilambilam, was publicly hanged behind the beach at Malay Bay as an 'example' to other Western Arnhem Landers.[2] This event had a great impact on the northwestern Arnhem communities and 'the people still talk about what happened' (Lamilami 1974:75). Thus, it was in these times of great change and challenge to the people's capacity to accommodate increasingly rapid change that Namadbara grew up.

Namadbara spent much of his life in the northwestern Arnhem region. He grew up in the Country of Iwaidja and Amurdak speakers between Cooper Creek and the Cobourg Peninsula, where both his mother and his father's clan estates are located. In his later life, he had camps at various places along the coast of Mountnorris and Malay bays, as well as at Murgenella. A favoured camping ground, however, was on his father's Country at Mangulwan near Mt Permain. He also spent significant periods of his life at both Gunbalanya (Oenpelli) and on Croker Island (Minjilang), where he is remembered as providing decisive community leadership in the context of the difficult changes and challenges the community was facing in coming to terms with settled mission life. It was at Oenpelli in the late 1940s that the anthropologists Ron and Catherine Berndt first met Namadbara and his classificatory brother Wilambilam (also regarded as clever). They observed and described healing sessions in which these two powerful Western Arnhem Land marrkidjbu were involved (Berndt & Berndt 1951; Berndt 1964). Ningoldie Blyth, Namadbara's brother's daughter, said, 'Everybody looked on them [Namadbara and Wilambilam] as leaders, because they were strong — strong in decision-making.'

Namadbara grew up at a time when non-Aboriginal entrepreneurs were seeking opportunities in this particular region. They required plentiful Aboriginal labour for the viability of their enterprises. In providing the labour needed, Western Arnhem Landers became experienced at the type of work required by

Europeans,[3] particularly those on this northwestern fringe. Namadbara spent frequent periods during his life engaged in enterprises and industries that these entrepreneurs and, later, government agencies brought to this western fringe of Arnhem Land — the buffalo shooting and skinning industry, trepang collecting, crocodile shooting, timber milling, road building and forestry.[4] He, along with a number of his countrymen, was closely associated with Reuben Cooper's series of timber mills[5] that operated principally during the period between the First and Second World Wars on the Cobourg Peninsula and in the Murgenella district of northwestern Arnhem Land (Lamilami 1974:84).

During this time Namadbara received the European name Paddy and, from the wife of Reuben Cooper, Sally Koosney Ah Mat, the nickname 'Compass'. Namadbara is said to have been given this name because of his extraordinary and unerring ability to find his way through featureless bush directly to any pre-arranged point. This was an ability that was considered by his countrymen to be beyond their normal bushcraft.

During the Second World War, he spent some time at Oenpelli. After the War, he resumed seasonal work, working for a time with Ernest Lake in his timber and buffalo operations at Maliyirrulk near Mt Permain, and later for other entrepreneurs who had begun trading in buffalo skins. Paddy Compass was said to have been an excellent shot and hunted buffalo on horseback. When the buffalo season was over, the Aboriginal workers would go crocodile shooting and then return to either Croker Island or Oenpelli. When the roads were being built in the Murgenella district, Namadbara worked on this enterprise and is said to have been instrumental in the surveying and selecting of the most appropriate routes for the new roads.

At Croker Island in the 1960s, he, along with painters such as Yirrwala and Midjaw-midjaw, produced a significant body of bark paintings — possibly stimulated by the interest in the subject shown by the Berndts and by the visiting Czech art collector and ethnologist Karel Kupka, who commissioned images of sorcery and magic (Caruana 1993:28). Namadbara's paintings of human, spirit and sorcery figures stand apart from the work of his fellow painters by their dynamic sensuousness and the remarkable sinuous and fluid movement of the figures depicted.[6] His paintings are held in a number of art galleries and collections around the world and included in a number of texts (e.g. Kupka 1972; Caruana 1993; Berndt, Berndt & Stanton 1982; Berndt & Berndt 1988; O'Ferrall 1990).

Namadbara was a man of great ceremonial and ritual knowledge and had achieved the highest ceremonial status. In keeping with the ceremonial traditions of this region, he had 'been right through' the Morak, Ubarr (Wuwalk), Marrayin and Lorrkon ceremonial cycles. As one man, Big Bill Neidjie, commenting on his ceremonial knowledge, said:

'Two Mimi Spirits (males) dancing' by Paddy Compass Namadbara, Croker Island, 1963. Image supplied by NMA.

'Maam, malignant spirit' [male figure with multiple arms and legs] c. 1963 by Paddy Namadbara. Image supplied by NGA. Note: Maam, the equivalent Iwaidja term to the Kunwinjku Nakidjkidj.

Well, we bin really believe and prove properly things [in those days] . . . no more half-half. So that Nabulanj [Namadbara's subsection identity — skin] im bin savvy anything, no matter what bit.

Big Bill's statement here could be loosely translated as: 'In those days (pre Second World War) we were fully committed to our ceremonies, demanding total discipline and our full attention. So Namadbara had a thorough grounding in and understanding of all our ceremonial cycles.' Bill compared the situation of more recent years unfavourably with those times.

Another ceremony that Namadbara was involved with was the Kunabibi ceremony, which did not come into the northwest Arnhem Land area until Namadbara was a middle-aged man. He went to 'Mr Berndt's Kunabibi' at Oenpelli in the early 1950s. He had not seen this ceremony before 'because', said Bill Neidjie, 'topside, belonga Beswick side' [it came from or belongs to the people of the southern and central Arnhem Land plateau region, around Beswick — a small Aboriginal community situated southeast of Katherine].[7]

As a young Ubarr initiate in his mid-teenage years, Namadbara is said to have spent four years in ceremonial seclusion, followed almost immediately by a further four years — at the Ubarr that was held at the Malay Bay Ubarr site in northwestern Arnhem Land. It is said that 'he came out really skinny' after this seclusion.

However, the account of his life that follows is principally from the point of view of his particular and extraordinary clever abilities, and how, according to the Western Arnhem Landers on whose accounts this story is based, he used these abilities to their benefit.

Making of a Clever Man —
Acquiring the Power

Western Arnhem Landers consider that the marrkidjbu derives his clever abilities from a special experience that he has endured after which he is no longer like an ordinary person. He now has marrngkidj, power which enables him to perceive events invisible to others. Another word for this power is mankordang, so a Kunwinjku 'doctor' is also called a na-kordang-yi — a man with magical power.[8]

The sugarbag event

Namadbara's initial encounter with the spirit world — at least the encounter which set him apart from others and during which people consider he was 'made' into a clever man — occurred when he was still a young man, perhaps in his late 20s. This account is generalised from the accounts of three different people, Bluey Ilkgirr, Thompson Yuludjiri, and Robert Djorlom. Each of these accounts agree in the basic outline of what happened, and differ mainly in that one may add some details that another lacks.

Namadbara was out hunting by himself one day.[9] It was along Cooper Creek, near a rockhole known as Kurrambalkwarrewong. He came across an antbed [termite mound] in which he thought there might be some sugarbag[10] so he stuck the end of his woomera, or shovel nose spear, to see if there was anything there, but there was nothing. 'No sugar egg, no mankung'. Instead, 'all the fly [bees] went out and bite him. Im too cheeky, that sugarbag!' They swarmed all over him and bit him from head to foot.[11] 'Bite him, he dropped, dropped unconscious.'

'Maam, malignant spirit' c. 1963 by Paddy Namadbara. Image supplied by NGA.

He lay there unconscious all that night until the afternoon of the next day. Bluey put it this way: 'Well, im bin finish that Old Man, im bin die. Im bin die there. He bin sleep one day, one night.' He finally woke up and found he was in a totally different place to where he had been attacked by the sugarbag fly. He was lying in a waterhole half a day's walk away from the other place, with his woomera and spears and other equipment lying nearby. 'How did he get there?'

Thompson Yuludjiri says that they were not really bees at all, or sugarbag; it was all an illusion created by spirit beings:

'Somebody bin just make em up, that fly. Is not really one, that might be belong to ghost, spirit men.'

Meanwhile, Namadbara's family and relatives back at the camp had been out looking for him but had not been able to find him. Now he wandered back to the camp. They asked him, 'What's wrong with you, Nabulanj?' 'I don't know. What's wrong?' he replied. He had lumps all over his body, lumps that developed into weeping sores. He became a sick man. He lay down and went to sleep. He was 'asleep' for five days, 'never wake up'.[12]

While Namadbara was asleep, or unconscious, the spirits of previous clever people appeared before him.[13] 'All the clever they bin come out now.' Among them were his two fathers, Marrarna, the older of the two, and Djumu, his biological father (two brothers of the nakangila subsection and, as per the kinship system, each being called father by Namadbara). They had both been 'clever blokes' during their lives, Marrarna having been the more powerful. Namadbara didn't know where he was or what he was doing here or who this 'spirit mob' was. Marrarna came up to him to help him but at this stage, Marrarna was unable to communicate directly with Namadbara.

He couldn't tell im all about this mob here, people.[14] Well, they bin make im proper clever. His father [Marrarna], im bin make im proper clever.

After this, Marrarna woke his son up:

All right. That old man [Marrarna], as soon as im bin make em, im bin get up, that [Namadbara]. Im bin wake [up], that young fella — Old Paddy.

Marrarna could now speak to Namadbara:

'Hello', im bin talkim.

'Who you?'

'Me, your father! What happened? Im hittim you?'

[But Namadbara] he couldn't know which one bin killim.

'Well', [Marrarna] said, 'I bin come up, your father, me.'

Marrarna is asking his son how he came to get into the spirit world — 'Did one of those spirits knock you out?' ['kill', 'hit' — that is, put him into a state where he can effectively communicate with the spirits and be made 'clever'. 'I bin come up' means 'I appeared to you'.]

They spoke together using a language peculiar to the spirit world. When they had finished talking, Marrarna said to him:

'You go on and go back home now, I'm going.' And that old man, father one, Nakangila, im bin go back now. But spirit![15]

Bluey Ilkgirr's account also includes the following event:

Then the marrwakani ['cheeky' yam] spirits came up to Namadbara singing their songs. 'Well that, they call marrwakani. Well, that devil-devil now — that spirit mob. Well, they come up singing, belong [to] im now.[16] They bin make im wake up.'

Namadbara was now possessed with clever abilities. But he did not tell anybody at this stage.

Soon after this, just after the sores had healed, he had to make a trip east to the Liverpool River, several days' walk away, to take an old man, another nabulanj, back to his Country. He left the old man there and made the return journey by himself, walking along the coast part of the way. He was walking along a beach around Junction Bay, in the Namarrabandja clan's estate Karabu, when he met two children. They were in fact spirit children[17] — two boys, one a little bigger than the other, and they made Namadbara their friend. They were described by Thompson Yuludjiri as:

Proper namarnde. Really. Not like us when we die [not dead people's spirits, which are sometimes also called namarnde]. No, not that one. [But] properly namarnde, really. Really.[18]

These namarnde accompanied Namadbara on his trip back home and stayed with him all his life. They were his spirit-helpers. He called them by the kin-term 'son' as they both were considered to belong to the nakodjok subsection, and also as his wurdwurd (children). Sometimes, others refer to them in English as Namadbara's 'friends'. It was through them that he was able to exercise his power. Thompson said:

That two little boy helped him heal — they gave him everything. That Old Man bin have power same way that two.

One man, Alan Randall, who spent some years growing up on Croker Island, recalls that one day he noticed some unfamiliar children playing around Namadbara's camp. He asked Jim Wauchope who these children were. 'They're not children you're seeing,' Jim replied, 'they're that Old Man's spirit-helpers.' Alan remembered them as having 'really shiny, healthy skin.'

Speaking with the yumbarrbarr

Big Bill Neidjie tells the story of Namadbara's further acquisition of power.[19] Like Namadbara, Big Bill spent much of his life working in the northwest Arnhem buffalo, crocodile and timber mill work camps and on the luggers that traded between them and Darwin. According to his own account, he was present at the work camp at the time that this event took place. It is clear from his accounts that Namadbara was the most significant mentor in his life.

Like the sugarbag event described above, this story also tells how Namadbara came to be in possession of such notable and special power. Bill Neidjie declares, '[Namadbara] was middle-aged, now he get close up old man, when he find his power'. Jacob Nayinggul (nakodjok), who as a teenager was taken under Namadbara's wing for some months after the death of Jacob's father in the late 1950s, thought that this shift was to a higher level of power, and came when 'he [Namadbara] was round about 50 — his early 50s.'[20]

This second account of the acquisition of Namadbara's powers, however, is not necessarily incompatible with the first. Rather, the two stories might well be considered as different episodes in the progressive acquisition and development of Namadbara's powers, in his developing career as a 'clever bloke'.

This event takes place near the Marralkiny timber mill camp, run by Joel Cooper's son, Reuben Cooper. Namadbara was walking alone one day in the bush. His attention was taken by a young stringybark tree:

'I went look, I turn around look, all smooth.' He said to himself, 'I'll sit down for a while, look this tree. This good tree.' He was sitting there all day.

Bill Neidjie tells this story, quite dramatically, as if Namadbara himself was speaking:

And this leaf [of the tree] was working, like that [demonstrates, rapidly shaking his hand] and now — my feeling he was changing with that tree.

I think he [the tree] teach me. 'You don't have to fight, you don't have to worry [about] anything.'

But, I don't know how, my mind, everything bin change, find meself change. I never speak, only that tree he was moving, but I feel it myself, he was changing [my] body.

Just about dark — I feel it behind, somebody walking, you know. I never look back, but I feel it somebody. Say you or somebody else, if you sit down [and] you don't look back, you sit, but you feelem that man coming? Well, I bin do that.

Orright, that man, he came, he hold my shoulder [from behind]. He was calling me, that man. I never look back. But he made me sit quiet, think about it. And all these feelings bin changed, my feelings. And that man, he was telling me, 'You good, you don't have to fright, you don't have to run away, or what. When I go home, you start walk home.' He said, 'Dark now'. He said, 'I'm going, what about you go home? When you go home, just sleep.'

And he went home.

At the time, Namadbara did not tell anybody what had happened to him. In Big Bill's account, immediately following this story, however, he tells of how Namadbara cured his brother (Dick Wilambilam nabulanj) of a sickness by extracting the object causing the sickness from inside his brother's body. He held it up showing everybody, saying, 'Here, look! This thing, he oughta kill you. He bin killim you close. But now he jump out. This the one.'

The 'man' who approached and spoke to Namadbara in the above account, and whom Namadbara comes to speak of as a 'friend' (in Bill's words), turns out to be a yumbarrbarr (a usually malicious spirit).[21] Yumbarrbarr, apparently, had been woken up in some way by the interaction going on between Namadbara and the tree. In Bill's account of the incident, this Yumbarrbarr explains to Namadbara:

'That tree he was talking to you, and that tree, he just like phone. I come from rock — I bin sleep orright, but that sing[ing out] bin wake me up.'

But Old Man [Namadbara], he said, 'I never sing out. I never say, "Hey! You mob!" I was sitting quiet.

But that tree im bin ring up, bin sing out — im bin pick up that man. He was a big man, big arms and big shoulders— like a gorilla.'

'Anytime, if you want me [Yumbarrbarr concludes] — if you want me, that tree, sit down again longa that tree — you might pick me up.'

Bill wanted to know how Namadbara would be able to 'pick up' the man again:

'I can pick im up anytime,' Namadbara answered him, 'I know that man, but you mob — you might run away. If you stay, all the kids, they might scream.'

But Namadbara, in Bill's account, did at some point demonstrate to the rest of them the 'picking up' of Yumbarrbarr:

He said, 'All right you mob, you don't believe, you look that tree there. Night-time you can look.'

'What [are we going to] see?'

'I don't know — what?'

[It's] dark now.

He bin sit down. And he said, 'Hey, you mob ready?'

And we look there, like spotlight, eh? — that light.

'Who put [that] light there?'

He said, 'What [did I tell you] now, you look!'

[It was] bright!

He said, 'That my friend, he can't come closer. You mob go look.'

Nah. We bin fright — some fellas, they bin fright.

'But he good man,' Namadbara reassured them, 'He can't kill [won't harm you].

But, ohh, he got power! That fella got power.'

In Big Bill's understanding, Namadbara considered that this particular power that he had [to call up the power of Yumbarrbarr] came through the tree. He explained to Bill that he did not get this power directly through his own efforts nor did he get it directly from another clever man, 'no one bin make me this power', but that the tree was the source:

I said [to Namadbara], 'Hey, what this power? What he bin do? Make yourself something?'

He said, 'Nah. My boy, only that tree. Tree bin give me power. That's all.'[22]

After he got this power, or 'found out' about it as it was described, he changed. 'All his feelings were changed,' Bill says of him. He was transformed in some essential way. Now he had no heart for fighting:

He didn't like fight, argument, he didn't like em. He change.

If, as a younger man, he had been ready with a spear and stick to fight, now he was changed. Bill has him saying:

'Myself, I was a bit too rough before. [People] fighting each other — brother killing one another [with] stick. I was young. Soon as I find out about this one here [the tree experience], I can't. I no more like [fighting, violence].'

[The tree taught him that] 'You don't have to fight, you don't have to worry, [or] anything.'

Put in this way, the experience clearly had a revelatory impact on Namadbara.

Since Namadbara already had some clever powers at this point in his life, as the details presented in the sugarbag event show, then this later experience with power can be seen as a step up the ladder towards the status, so clearly achieved in the eyes of his fellow Western Arnhem Landers, of being a 'properly number one marrkidjbu'.

That such a progression indeed took place is also suggested in Jacob Nayinggul's account. He had heard that, as a younger man, Namadbara had been just [an ordinary] marrkidjbu:

. . . with just healing sort of sources — power — just healing power he had. But not this. [This was] something stronger — different.

What 'this' is will emerge as this account of Namadbara's life progresses. At this point, it includes a power and vision for the future of the community rather than simply the individual.

The Power of the Marrkidjbu

A young Gunbalanya man who spoke in general about the practices of marrkidjbu, considered that their functions could be categorised into three: healing, sorcery and kumula, which he translated as 'giving purpose to that job', 'giving power to people who might ask for it, [a power that enhances] their skills'. He said, 'It might be anything from, say, playing football to learning English, or any desired skill.'

Kumula: Giving purpose for that job

Jacob Nayinggul, a prominent elder and leader within the Gunbalanya community, remembered Namadbara's influence on himself and on the wider community, essentially through this kumula.

One day, when Jacob was still a teenager and being looked after by Namadbara, they were out hunting together on the lower Cooper Creek looking for crocodile eggs. Their dogs put a feral cat up a tree. Namadbara told Jacob to spear it. He did so reluctantly. The cat was growling as Jacob went up to it, put his foot on its head, took out the spear and then, under Namadbara's instructions, cut open the side of the cat and took out some fat. By this time the cat was just about dead. They left the cat lying there at the side of the river near the bank; Namadbara said to stand back. He told Jacob to sit down, 'watch the cat, don't move, don't blink, don't scratch or do anything,' and instructed him to keep his hands firmly cupped over his testicles. The Old Man then went forwards and backwards, forwards and backwards, several times — heavy footed, bent kneed — from the river bank towards the cat and back again. From out of the river and up from behind the Old Man's back came a willy-willy [whirlwind]. It went straight to the cat — 'phht!' — and then continued on past Jacob.[23] The Old Man now told him to go up to the cat. When he did so, 'the cat got up, groggy, groggy, and then suddenly [to Jacob's astonishment] jumped up and climbed back up the tree, just like a wild cat again.'[24] A willy-willy is one of the forms in which a clever person may manifest power; in this case, the willy-willy was later said actually to be a manifestation of a ngalyod, a Rainbow Serpent. At other times, this power may be manifested through the activity or agency of the spirit-helpers, or again, through the manipulation of the power-objects within the clever person's body.

It was back at Oenpelli two or three months after this incident that Jacob ran into Namadbara again. Namadbara asked him what he wanted to do with his life. Jacob's father had died not long before and he was now leaving the bush where he had grown up to come for the first time into the Oenpelli mission settlement. He was in his mid-teens, a late starter at school, and consequently a long way behind the other younger students in school abilities, especially in English. So, he told Namadbara he wanted to learn at school and especially to learn to speak English. Namadbara said, 'Mah [OK], we'll do it!' And he brought out a little wooden object carved from a piece of milkwood tree. It had a hollow in it. Jacob described the whole thing as a 'radio'. In the hollow was some of the cat fat (kun-balem) that had come from their previous hunting trip. The wooden object, also referred to by Jacob as 'kundulk',[25] was now imbued with its power. Jacob was instructed to take two specially prepared short lengths of hard fencing wire, heat them in the fire until they were red hot, stick them into the kunbalem and, at the same time, talk into the 'radio', putting into it his words about what he wanted for his future. Namadbara told him he would receive the power to succeed in his undertakings. And so it happened. Jacob soon surpassed the other students at school and before too long was a teacher himself. He attributes his consequent success to this beginning.

In Jacob's account, Namadbara says to him:

'Yeah. All right, we'll get you in there [to school].'

And — it happened.

First I went to school — but too old — than the others. Teacher said, 'Bit older than the other kids, but we can teach you,' she said.

I went to school every night and she taught me — English. And from there I picked it up.

Then one day the Principal came and offered me a job as assistant at the shop. I was just put there automatically. And then one of the Mission teachers said if I wanted to be a teacher. And from there it went on and on and on.

And a couple of times he saw me, talked to me. Said, 'Oh, you're getting there all right! You'll get somewhere, long way.'

And it all happened in his time, while he was still alive.

Healing — defeating namorrorddo

For Thompson Yuludjiri, one of the most significant demonstrations of Namadbara's power was when, after a long, long struggle, he succeeded in defeating a namorrorddo that had been continually stealing Namadbara's sick wife's kunmalng (soul, breath, vital-force). Namadbara's last wife, Ngalkangila (Rhoda), had become sick through an attempt of murnde on her – a form of sorcery, which involves heating or 'roasting' an article of clothing or bodily waste belonging to the victim.[26] Namadbara's ability to cure his wife was convincing evidence to Thompson that Namadbara was stronger, more powerful than anybody else, because 'that Old Man, he had same power [as] any namorrorddo!'

IAN: How did you know that he was stronger?

OK. I will tell you.

When that Ngalkangila there — she was very sick — [because] somebody bin roast [her]. [It happened] at Imbalmun [one of the Cooper family timber mills on the Cobourg Peninsula]. And we went across to Croker [Thompson was living with them as a son]. She had [Western] medicine, but she couldn't get better.

Orright. This Old Man, he want to fix im up, this one [his wife, Ngalkangila].

Orright. He put string across [from one tree to another tree].

And she was very sick. And that namorrorddo, he bin coming underground to grab her kunmalng. He grabbed that, not her body, but kunmalng; what we are now, like if kunmalng go away, well, we finish! But that Old Man, he know that namorrorddo there, he grabbed that kunmalng back.

That namorrorddo bin try, try, try — nothing. Well, that namorrorddo bin coming underground to grab kunmalng, but that Old Man, he saw that namorrorddo underground and make im to go away.

IAN: Can you kill namorrorddo, or just make them go away?

Just make them go away, or get that kunmalng back. And he gave it to that olguman [old woman] — gave it back — that kunmalng.

IAN: What happen if that namorrorddo bin take that kunmalng and take im away, what happen?

Finish! She gonna die! Once that namorrorddo kill that kunmalng then you will finish.

IAN: And that string?

Yeah. Might be clever one — clever string he had there. He tied [between] two tree, then every night he bin walking up and down, on the beach [at Croker Island]. Well, that Old Man bin helping every night. Every night! I seen it! When I bin wake, I see that Old Man walk around longa bush. And walk up and down, like that [demonstrates] and that olguman, his wife. We was camping with them. And when I got up, I [would] see that Old Man — up and down. On that beach, he was walk around, back and forward, back and forward all the way [along the string]. I seen it. To make that old woman to come back alive again.[27]

He bring that kunmalng back, and she bin run away — not her body, but that kunmalng. That Old Man bin looking around, grab it, bring it back here — run away again. Because she was very sick. She got skinnier and skinnier.

IAN: And how long was that old woman sick?

Long time! Might be, one year.

IAN: And when he got that kunmalng back, she got better?

Better! All the way! But might be that namorrorddo . . . That Old Man, he had same power of any namorrorddo.

IAN: So he was stronger than namorrorddo?

Yeah. Stronger. He had power too!

Thompson Yuludjiri explained further:

But that kunmalng, like with me and you, it's here, inside. But if that kunmalng go away, you drop! Dead! That's what that Old Man told me. Im bin tell me everything [about] namorrorddo taking kunmalng. [So] one day, might be afternoon, if that namorrorddo take your kunmalng there, put it — then as soon as he kill [it], then where you [your body] laying down there — [you] finish. No more wind. Finish.

One namorrorddo, when we [are very] sick, he come along — you can't see im. He might be standing long way, he push that small string — like a cotton, and grab [your] kunmalng.

IAN: You can't see that string?

No, you can't. 'Clever' string. Can't see.

IAN: That string . . . it belongs to namorrorddo?

That namorrorddo, 'clever' one. OK, grab [your] kunmalng, take it [to his] home, leave it there. When he go hunting, he will leave you there — that kunmalng — [at his home], and you're there [your body at your own home], very sick, still alive — he don't kill you yet. When the time come, soon as that namorrorddo kill you kunmalng, and that home where you [are] sick . . . finish. Dead. That what story Old Man told me.'[28]

Another successful healing undertaken by Namadbara, also a defeat of a namorrorddo attempting to steal a kunmalng, was recounted by Thompson Yuludjiri about a Djok man. This man, a member of the Djok kunmokurrkurr, had been speared right through his body, from the back of his neck through to his chest. This spearing took place at Gunbalanya sometime after the Second World War. The man's wife found him lying 'dead' in a pool of blood when she returned home to their house one night. She called out for the Old Man. Namadbara came, sent her away back to his own camp, while he stayed there all night and worked on the victim:

And that Old Man, he was there all night, all night [until] daylight — to fix that man up.

IAN: Oh, he tried to fix im up?

He bin fix im up! Yes. Him bin fix im up. Fix im up. Bimarnbom [healed]. And he came back live again. And that's [the] way he got kill[ed] for.

[Afterwards, the victim] got bruise [scar] top of the neck [Thompson indicates the size of a fingertip].

And yoh, he fix im up. Fix im orright.

But, maybe that kunmalng, im bin takem namorrorddo [i.e. namorrorddo stole the kunmalng]. And [Namadbara] bin follow that namorrorddo and bringim back that kunmalng. Might be! But I don't know. Because he know how to go, and he know that namorrorddo grab kunmalng. He always know.

Thompson is explaining that, as part of healing the overall trauma of the physical spear wound, Namadbara was skilled enough to retrieve the victim's soul, his kunmalng, from the namorrorddo and thus bring the victim back from otherwise certain death.

These first two episodes involved Namadbara retrieving the stolen 'soul' of the patient. Other episodes given as instances of Namadbara's successful healing activity involved his extracting 'sickness objects' from a sorcery victim — objects that are considered to have been deliberately projected into a person, either by sorcery or through 'wrong action' on the part of the person.

Bark painting 'Namorrordo, malicious spirit of the Stone Country' by Charlie Najombolmi, Balawurru. Photo: Jason McCarthy, National Museum of Australia. Image supplied by NMA.

Removing 'sickness objects'

Shorty Dirdi, who spent many years of his working life with 'Old Man Compass', tells how he was healed by Namadbara on one occasion. It was at a camp at Ngalkiwudj, close to Mangulwan, that the Old Man healed him. He took out a little black stone covered in blood from the side of Shorty's stomach. Shorty's father, who was with him at the time, had gone to Namadbara to ask him to help his son, and he was there when Namadbara pulled the stone out and showed everybody. It was early in the morning, 'about 6 o'clock'.

'He'll be better next morning — you can go hunting [together] then,' Namadbara told them.

He'd pull out bone, or hair, or something, show im [to the patient and onlookers], and chuck im in water — always chuck im in water. He always show im [to the onlookers] — bone, or something.[29]

In another account of removal of a sickness object, Bill Neidjie tells of how, sometime after Namadbara had 'the tree experience' and about which he had not yet told anybody, he went home to find his brother Dick Wilambilam sick, 'close up, finish' [nearly dead]:

Im bin go sit down on top of his chest. I was watching im. His brother nearly finished. He sit longa his chest — brother — his own brother. I was watching. What he do? I don't know. That man might be im finish — crook [ill]. And he sit there, might be two or three hour. Or might be six hour. He was sitting down on top of him. Next minute his brother, he move. He was moving. And that boy, his brother, he bin get up. Him bin get up, stretch his legs. [Namadbara] bin tellim im, 'Turn around, look! I look you[r] back.' Him bin turn around look [at] his back. He said, 'He's all right. [When I] sleep, I see this thing here, like stone. He was inside your body.'

But how he jump out? He never pull im out.

He said, 'He jump out last night. That why I show you everybody. Here, look! This thing, he oughta kill you. He bin killim you close. But now he jump out. This the one.'

We seen it, every one of us. Hard one. Black.

'What we do?' [they ask Namadbara]. 'We gotta burn im [the object], or what?'

'Nah. Chuck im longa mud. It's all right then.'

'Why don't you burn im?'

'No, you kill that man. If you burn im, you gotta go kill that fella there. More better chuck im longa cool country, you know, mud.'

They bin take em, bury im longa mud.

That boy, he was all right.

And Bill concluded his account of this episode, 'But ohh, that's the bloke now, eh? He had power!'

The common technique among 'regular' Western Arnhem Land marrkidjbu is to apply the lips to the skin of the patient at the affected part (where the sickness object is perceived to be) and to suck (ngordmang),[30] extracting blood and the sickness object in the process, although the skin is not broken. However, those of Namadbara's calibre had such power that they did not need to do this.[31]

For Bluey Ilkgirr, one of the impressive features of Namadbara's practice — and indicative of his particular degree of power as a marrkidjbu — was the fact that he didn't have to 'suck' in order to extract the sickness-causing object from a patient.

IAN: And if, like someone was sick, he [Namadbara] might — ngordmey?

Yeah — ngordmangi — but couldn't [did not need to] do that.

Only im just puttim finger, and im bin take em out [extracted sickness objects].

IAN: But he didn't do that [sucking]?

No. No to do that.

IAN: Didn't have to?

No.

IAN: You bin look?

Yeah! Many people! And that Old Man couldn't [didn't need to] touch im that his body, that dead fella one. And that Old Man, clever man, couldn't touch im. Nah. Im just look and touch im with finger.

IAN: He didn't have to touch im?

No. He couldn't have to touch im and ngordmey, larrh [no, no need to suck].

IAN: Because he was too clever?

Too clever! Only his finger. And im bin take em out there, look.

IAN: And what was it that he took out?

Kabbay (ironwood resin), or burrdjang (cloth, material) — or djalwarr (trouser material). They bin all gonna kill that man or that girl.

And im bin look that same one [as an] X-ray [He could 'see' the sickness-causing object in the patient's body, just as a modern X-ray can see into the body].

IAN: And he showed you the object?

Yeah. Him bin show em everyone. Showed em. [Then] soaked em, or what. No more bury em, but soak em.

But im too clever, that one.

Today? No one clever. Everybody sick? [Then they go to hospital in] Darwin. That's the doctor there.

X-ray? Im bin see always [like an] X-ray — night-time, afternoon time, morning time.

The usual time for a marrkidjbu to examine a patient so as to 'see' inside for any sickness object is when the sun is low in the sky — later afternoon or early morning, and sometimes by moonlight — when the patient stands against the light and the marrkidjbu can use his 'vision' to carry out the diagnosis.

Him bin look [at] that boy, im bin say, 'Nah, you're all right. You good. Little bit, you were going to die, but you good now. And you come back afternoon, or morning time, next day, I'll see you again.'

Go back again, and im bin go and look, 'Nothing. No [thing] inside. Good.'

And im bin chuck im, whole lot [throws away any sickness object extracted]. I dunno what im bin do [I can't explain how he was able to do it]. Im too clever, like a doctor too [practitioner of Western medicine].

Im can't look, eh? [A Western doctor can't see into a sick person's body without special equipment]. You can't look. Even me, I can't look!

That doctor [marrkidjbu], I dunno, by spirit, by X-ray. Just like glass. Well, same way Old Man, like glass. You know that X-ray, eh? Well, same way [that the marrkidjbu can see]. [But] this Balanda one [X-ray machine], that [an] outside one.

You [yourself] can't see that way. But this Old Man, he could just [use his] eye. That's all. Him bin just go — [demonstrates, using his eyes to look into you]. Just look, didn't, couldn't, [didn't need to] say anything, im bin just look in the body, [with] eye. That's all.

Like Balanda [Western doctor], im different. [But] Bininj, im bin just look that eye.[32]

Healing himself

Thompson Yuludjiri gives an account of an incident, told to him by Namadbara, in which Namadbara successfully healed himself through the agency of his two 'spirit-men'. It was at Gunbalanya sometime after the 'last world war' (1945).

Namadbara was camping with another man in the pandanus near the billabong, at the Arrkuluk end of the settlement:

And one man bin sneak up with his spear and kill [hit, strike] Nabulanj.

Just here on the back. And he yell out — 'arrgh!'

And that bloke [his camping partner] bin listen. 'What's wrong?'

'Somebody bin kill me.'

And that morning he was biggest sick. Sick. He got skinny. And that two little boy, spirit-men had come back, watch him and help him to fix im up. Fix im up, fix im up.

Might be one week, he was all right. He got up.

And that man [that had] killed [speared] him — [Namadbara knew who it was]. Him turn now.

He called that two spirit-men to come that night to help him and sneak up and kill him.

So, that bloke dead, this old bloke live.

Old Man didn't start it.

Him bin start it!

He told me that story about that. And he showed me that lump here [at the back of his neck], he had lump.

Healing — Balanda accounts

The anthropologists Ronald and Catherine Berndt, in their visits to Western Arnhem Land from the late 1940s to the late 1960s, knew and worked with both Namadbara and his nabulanj brother, Wilambilam. To provide a contemporary Western perspective on Namadbara's healing procedures and his marrkidjbu work, Catherine Berndt's account of two healing incidents involving the brothers is included.

The first incident involves a young man who took ill one cold season in the late 1940s and who, instead of recovering, gradually became worse. One of the young man's relatives:

. . . sent for old Namadbara and his brothers [including Wilambilam], who came with their wives. They built up the fire, covered him with a blanket, and got water for him. Old Namadbara moved the women and children aside: 'Give me room!' They moved quickly. He came close to the patient and touched him, while Wilambilam touched his feet. They 'felt' him all over. Then they told the women, 'Get hot water, and bathe him now and then. Don't use cold water, and don't keep on bathing him, or he'll become worse. Bathe him now and, when the sun is rising, bathe him again. We'll come back soon and "heal" him again. After that he will be well. It will take three days.' They 'felt' him again and repeated, 'Don't cry, he'll be all right, in maybe three days.'

The patient slept quietly, for a long time, while Namadbara and his brothers 'watched over' his spirit, guarding it, putting it back into his body. After a time he woke and asked, 'Who were those two men touching me? . . . I saw two men in my dream . . . washing my body with very cold water, making me feel well again. I don't know where we were: somewhere up in the sky perhaps. I don't know that place, it was a different place altogether, where those powerful men always go.' From that point he grew stronger and, in a few weeks, he was quite well again (Berndt 1964:275).

In the second incident, a young woman had died, leaving a baby daughter to be looked after by her sister and her mother. The baby fretted and cried continuously. The matter led to a series of recriminations in the camp and very strained relationships as a result of accusations and counter-accusations between the two women and between the other relatives:

At last [the sister's husband] called in old Namadbara and Wilambilam to help. When the two men came, they stood 'listening' attentively for a time, without speaking, then moved around, still 'listening'. Presently they reported the reason for the child's crying: Her dead mother was crying too, wandering about the camp in search of her, trying to take her away to the land of the dead. 'Her ghost is here with you', they told [the two women]. 'She wants her child. Take the child, build up a big fire of ironwood leaves, with plenty of smoke. Hold the child close beside it, don't leave her away from the fire. Then the mother won't be able to seize her for fear of burning her hands. And you two women, don't cry. Let her ghost go quietly away. Look after the child. You are her own mother's mother and her "mother". Care for her, so that the ghost can depart, leaving the child behind with you, in your charge . . . '

They underlined the dependence of the child, its need for affection and care, and the two women's joint responsibility for its welfare now that its mother . . . had left it in their keeping. [The] advice did not immediately resolve the trouble [but] it came at a strategic point, at the peak of the crisis; after it, [the two women] gradually became more 'settled', quieter . . . (Berndt 1964:276).

Sorcery

According to all accounts, Namadbara would have nothing to do with the practice of sorcery. Big Bill said that he would tell him, 'That's silly',[33] in effect saying, 'Don't get mixed up in that, it will rebound on you':

You don't want that mankarni and all that — he killing you [it will end up killing you].

Mankarni is a form of sorcery that involves knocking out the victim, making an incision and taking blood from their neck, inserting grass into the body cavity, and then reviving the victim.[34] Bill recalled an incident to illustrate Namadbara's attitude to mankarni. Once when they were at 'the Timbermill', Namadbara observed that 'a Liverpool River man' had been the victim of mankarni. In Bill's words, Namadbara says:

'See that man sitting down there? He got hole longa his body. That clever — fuckin' mankarni.'

Namadbara's wife, Ngalkangila, went and told the victim who, despite her advice, didn't believe her.

Two days later, he got sick.

[Namadbara's wife urged Namadbara]: 'You go make im, fix im up, poor thing.'

[But Namadbara refused to interfere.] He said, 'Me, I don't like [to get involved]. That's his business. They killim? That's their business. Me? I never like killing people. I want clean. And mankarni, silly.'

At another time he advised Bill to keep away from sorcery business:

He told me, 'That mankarni — you savvy 10 Commandments, Roman? [Well] that kind — that wicked.'

'No more killim people — that wicked.'

'If you see devil, you gonna see another devil, you gotta see another devil. No good. Forget that one. Keep away altogether.'

That true [Bill comments]. Uncle didn't like it. Corroboree, he wanted. Corroboree, corroboree.

'I wantem corroboree,' [he would say], all the time.

Thompson also recalls him saying, 'That's silly', in reference to the use of sorcery power against people. Namadbara also had sole access and control over a major Western Arnhem Land 'sickness' site on his Country at Lanka. Thompson said he could have used his power 'to send that sickness' against anyone or any group he wished to have revenge on. But he told Thompson that he had no wish to kill people. 'That's silly,' Namadbara said.

Namadbara's brother's daughter, Ningoldie Blyth, says that he and Wilambilam always taught them 'not to treat people badly, not to say harsh things'. She says that, while growing up at Gunbalanya, she never heard anybody claim that Namadbara or Wilambilam were doing anything bad (practising sorcery) against anybody. 'People would come and wake them up in the middle of the night to come and help somebody. They were always known to heal people.'

Manifestations of Power

The power of a clever person may manifest itself in a number of forms. It can be in the form of a willy-willy, said to be a manifestation of a ngalyod; at other times, it might be through the activity or agency of the spirit-helpers or, again, through the manipulation of the power objects within the clever person's body. Other manifestations of power by Namadbara include his uncanny knowledge of the environment, and of events happening far away, beyond a normal ability to know.

Water divining

Jim Wauchope spent many years working with Namadbara at Cooper's timber mills and other enterprises on the Cobourg Peninsula and in the Murgenella region. For him, Namadbara was a major teacher. This story was told to me by Alan Randall as told to him many years previously by Jim Wauchope. I later read this account to Jim who confirmed the details:

One day Compass told him that there was water underground somewhere near and to go out and find it. They were working in a stony area and Jim considered that there was no water anywhere near. Anyway, he went out and criss-crossed the area, over and over again but could not find anything. Compass told him to keep on trying. Finally, he felt that as he rode past a certain tree, he would get a funny feeling each time. So, he decided to mark the tree, put a tape around it. Then he went and reported to the Old Man that he couldn't find any water, but that he had kept having this funny feeling around this tree. The Old Man praised him and said, 'Boy, you did well. There will be water gushing up high into the air from there.' Jim couldn't believe it, because it was such a high and stony area, not at all the area you might expect underground water to be in.

Anyway, two or three months later, a government water survey team came into the area, with a drilling rig. Jim told the foreman, who turned out to be a mate of his, to drill at the particular spot that Jim had previously found. The drill team settled down to drill. The foreman was a drinker, and he settled down to drink, and watch and wait, and offer appropriate comments. After the men had drilled perhaps 30 feet, they said to the foreman, 'It's no use, the ground is absolutely dry, the cores are dry — no evidence whatsoever.' However, the foreman, quite happily guzzling away and a bit sozzled by now, said, 'Keep on drilling!' He believed his mate Jim. So the men drilled on, but again still no evidence whatsoever. 'Keep on drilling!' Finally, a really deep hole had been drilled, but — no water.

Now, Jim had faith in old Compass's assessment and so was a bit puzzled and unsettled at this lack of a show. He went over and dropped a stone down the drill hole. Didn't make any noise. Then he noticed water slowly coming up the hole, not far from the surface. Soon it gushed out of the hole and high into the air.

The water was from a major artesian basin, Jim later said, and the Old Man had correctly predicted that water would be found there.

Namadbara and nature

An aspect of Namadbara's specialised knowledge was his ability to reveal aspects of the workings of the natural environment that were not apparent to others. This knowledge was clearly highly valued by Western Arnhem Landers. He had a deep understanding of and an affinity with nature such that others relied on him for advice. In terms of seasonal availability of animals and plant food, he provided advice on the best hunting strategies — when to go and when not to bother, where to go and what would be available. Ron Cooper recalls fishing with Namadbara:

You know, he could tell you — if you wanted water, he would tell you where the water was. If you wanted a bundle of fish, he would tell you when the fish would come. You know, years ago we used to go to Wak [Murgenella billabong]. He knew the time and date — when the time to poison that — not poison it, make them [fish] all come to the top. And my father — we'd get barrels and barrels of salt and then we'd go. And we'd get all the fish and then we'd salt all the fish, that was it. Finish.

IAN: And that Old Man would know — would tell you when to go?

When to go, yeah. What date? He would tell us the migration of the crayfish. They'd migrate along the beach. Thousands and hundreds — big. He would know what day it was. 'Today's the day to go and catch them.' And there would always be firesticks of paperbark — no netting — used to spear them and that. It was like — survival. At night [it took place]. He knew what time they would travel. You'd get paperbark, wrap it up, in the fire and light it, and then — spear them.

IAN: And he was right?

Always was right.

Jamesie Wauchope, Jim's eldest son, recounted how, at times when they were camped at one of their beach sites on Mountnorris Bay, he would often tell the Old Man that he was taking the boat out the next day fishing. On some occasions, however, the Old Man would say, 'No, don't go! Too rough tomorrow' — although to his own eye and weather understanding, there would be no hint of coming bad weather. 'And the next day it would be very rough,' recalled Jamesie.

Jamesie gave another account to highlight Namadbara's acute sensitivity to change in the bush. He commented on the fact that '30 years ago' (in the early 1960s), Namadbara spoke to him about some of the classic traditional 'flower indicators' of the Western Arnhem Land seasonal calendar. 'Flower indicators' is Jamesie's phrase for calendar plants — certain flowers or blossoms coming into bloom that indicate a particular animal is fat and ready for hunting or a plant is ripe and ready for harvesting. Namadbara told him that some were then 'out of sync', even though to others, they still appeared to be 'in sync'. Certainly no one else noticed any change. 'But now, it's quite obvious to all that they are quite out of sync due to the changes in the seasons and the environment,' Jamesie, an Indigenous Kakadu Park Ranger of long standing, concluded.

Clever knowledge

An aspect of Namadbara's abilities that particularly impressed itself on Jamesie Wauchope's memory were two demonstrations of Namadbara's knowledge of events happening at a distant place.

At one time, when Namadbara and Jamesie were camping on the beach at Coombe Point on Mountnorris Bay, Namadbara told him that the next day a boat would come from Croker Island — and he made the 'clutched claw' hand sign — the indication that someone had died. The next day, Jamesie was sitting on the beach looking out to sea when he noticed a small dot on the horizon gradually drawing closer. A boat from the direction of Croker was coming. The boat arrived and, sure enough, the person got out making the clutched claw sign, indicating that they should come to Croker and participate in mourning rituals. 'How did that Old Man know?' Jamesie commented.

The other example of Namadbara's ability to know of something occurring at a distance was also related by Jim Wauchope. Jim worked alongside Namadbara for many years in Cooper's timber mill camps and other associated enterprises in the Murgenella region. One night in his house at Murgenella, he woke up, very sick. A little while later, he said he was 'shocked' to find Namadbara had arrived from where he was camping in a donga (a small cabin) about 'a quarter of a mile away'. Namadbara had woken up knowing that Jim needed his help and had come. 'How did that Old Man know?' Namadbara then proceeded to 'fix him up'. The procedure included massage. By the end of that day, Jim was 'as right as rain'.

Another description of Namadbara's powers occurred when, years later, Ron Cooper returned from Darwin to Cobourg Peninsula, bringing his six sons to meet Namadbara for the first time. The Old Man astonished them all. He correctly identified each of the boys by name, though never having seen them before, and 'blessed' one of them in particular.

At the more mundane end of this display of abilities, Namadbara demonstrated to Big Bill Neidjie his powers, establishing that he was not like an ordinary person in this respect. He asked Bill to try to creep up on him when he was asleep at night. In Big Bill's words, Namadbara tells him:

'My feeling, he don't think about — my feeling [is] different.'

He said, 'If I sleep in the night I know you sneak up — but you can't find me.' He told me, 'You try sneak up. Come to me. I will sleep. No good you come early,' he said. 'You try! You gotta come, but something going to stop you.'

Well I bin get up. I bin try. But I bin walk very soft. Bin walk half way.

Something — man-like. [I] think about it, turn around. He said, 'Turn around and go back.' I said [to myself], 'Something [here], oh no good.' My feeling, you know, told me I better go back.

I went back.

Old Man said, 'What stopped you?'

I said, 'I don't know. You was watching me.'

'Of course I was watching you!' [through this 'something'].

'How's that?' [How do you do it?] I asked. 'How?' 'Can't you give me some [of this power]?' Bill asks him.

In saying to Bill, 'my feeling, he don't think about . . . ', Namadbara is describing his own state of mind or being. I interpret this sentence as: 'My mind or state of being, "feeling", is different to yours. Mine is not disturbed or distracted by rampant thoughts or feelings'.[35]

Jamesie Wauchope was also set the same task but equally without success.

The world of the dead

A very common feature of clever knowledge the world over is that its source is conceived as being in the world of the dead (e.g. Stephen 1995:160–161).[36] Dead people's spirits, particularly those of close relatives, provide advice and guidance through this realm and information about it is revealed under the tutelage of these spirit ancestors. One who has learnt to control their experiences of, or their interaction with, this realm of the dead gains a further avenue of ability to wield (supernatural) power.

According to the accounts which Namadbara gave to some of his countrymen, he had had such experiences through which he gained knowledge of this realm. From these experiences he was able to describe aspects of it. With the help of his deceased father's spirit and his two spirit-children, he made visits to this world. In Big Bill's account, Namadbara tells him something of this realm where Bill's deceased family members are, and which Namadbara had visited in dreams with the assistance of his father. He tells of its interface with the world of the living. Namadbara assured Bill that, after he has passed away, he will be there (in this unseen world) with his brothers and other family members, and it is from there that he may 'come out' into this world to 'give more story' to Bill, if Bill follows the proffered instructions. It is not entirely clear from the following account but it would appear that the conversation takes place in a vision or dream that Bill has. During this dream or vision, Namadbara and Bill's deceased wife appear to him:

'We'll be there' [Bill then explains who Namadbara means by 'we']: four nabulanj and one nangarridj and their daughter (my mother). Six altogether [plus] another uncle. That why that dream, he follow im.

'But, we all there,' he said. 'Your mother — she's there.'

'But what [should] I do?' [asks Bill].

'You can't do anything. We can't do anything too, we blocked up. You in outside, we in inside, but middle we blocked,' he said.

I said, 'How you know?'

'I know, I bin there.'

'Who took you there?' I said. 'You just bin walk in yourself?'

'No, your grandfa, he took me.'

IAN: His *father*?

Yeah.

'Everything there. But, you know, gate sitting down there — that man [a gatekeeper?], he wicked man,' he said. 'I don't like im.'[37] But I bin dream, last time,' he said, 'I watchim, this man.'

'But all [your] uncle[s] there — we might do something [i.e. manifest ourselves]. Your grandfa there, your mother [too]. But we gotta do something,' he told me.

He'll come, I'll dream [predicts Bill — of Namadbara reappearing to him from the world of the dead].

'I givem you story, and keep that story. Tell all the kids,' [Namadbara concludes].

However, Bill had not yet made the determination to go to Mangulwan (the site where he would have to go) to meet with Namadbara's spirit — Mangulwan, an extensive billabong, being the focal site of Namadbara's Alarrdju clan Country and where Namadbara's spirit is said to reside since his death.[38]

In another experience of the dead, Namadbara told Thompson of an occasion during which his two spirit-helpers 'took' him to view the body of a newly deceased person and where he saw events unfolding that an ordinary person would not be able to see. During this experience, Namadbara observed how the namorrorddo and the spirits of the deceased person's ancestors (namarnde) deal with the body and soul of the newly dead:

IAN: And did Nabulanj [Namadbara] talk about that namorrorddo?

Him reckoned he bin see im. The two wurdwurd [spirit-children] bin take im to see all the namorrorddo business [ceremony]. Only namorrorddo, not namarnde. No more. They bin have business, all those namorrorddo. Namarnde have [separate] business.

IAN: They got name for that business?

From dead man. Not the namorrorddo dead. Me! [The ceremony belongs to deceased humans]. Old Man reckons, first time [that] we takem that dead body and bury him there, and that night namorrorddo time, big mob namorrorddo. They come there to pickim up that dead body there, get im out, might be spirit. Get im spirit out, and they wait for another namorrorddo who can come with the light [not daylight but 'like a spotlight', as the bright light described in the earlier yumbarrbarr namorrorddo incident]. They come for the ceremony. That namorrorddo come there, he can get that meat out [flesh from the corpse], little bit — about that much [indicating small amount with his fingers]. [Each] namorrorddo have about that much meat. [The flesh is then taken home and 'roasted' and the small piece grows big, enough to feed the rest of the namorrorddo family].

Views of the extensive main billabong at Mangulwan where Namadbara's spirit is said to reside. Photo: Ian White.

First night [after death], namorrorddo come. Next day, namarnde come — big mob. They grab spirit. They come, all them family [ancestral ghosts, namarnde, of the deceased person] pick him up and take him. Finish.

IAN: Nabulanj told you this?

Yoh. He bin sneak up there. Him and that two kids bin sneak up there and watchim namorrorddo. Watchim namorrorddo, what they doing there. [But, Thompson explained, that Nabulanj and his spirit-children personally knew the man whose body is there, and sorrow overcomes them].

Nabulanj and that two kid, they know that man, [that] body, and they reckon, 'Come on, we better go — that man,' that two reckon. 'We bin sorry [for] that. More better we move away, we don't want to look. Because they cut im up.'

IAN: And then the second day the namarnde come? And what do they do?

They come up and dig him out again.

IAN: And they eat him?

No! They don't eat him! They dancing — corroboree. Do corroboree, finish, drink, ahhh. Spirit, take [the spirit] out, give em to family. He go to that family, and [they] take em back home.

IAN: His family?

You know, say, like my mother and all the family; my grandpa, or my father. He must be there, that second night. And as I die, they bury me there. Then, those people there waiting for me. They get me up. Those family walk down there, grab my arm, drag me [to] where they are.

IAN: All your family that's already dead, already finished? So all them spirit, they belong to your family?

Yeah. They come back for me now.

IAN: And take you with them?

Yoh. Mmm.

IAN: And Nabulanj and those two little ones, they bin see all this business?

Yoh. All that business. And the Old Man reckoned, that [at] namarnde time [the second night they viewed the event], he was there with [the namarnde ancestral ghosts]. And all that namarnde bin stop, you know, and this two friend[s] of his said, 'Hey, he [the dead man] same like you and me,' and everybody bin move now. All that namarnde, big mob, they nearly ran away.

IAN: Because they saw Namadbara watching?

Because they saw him, that Old Man there. 'That old fella there [the deceased], he's like you and me' [Namadbara is also in spirit form, like the namarnde and the newly deceased]. He [the deceased] start move now, see corroboree and dancing and all that. And he [Namadbara] saw them. He was there!

Big Bill describes a similar encounter experienced by Namadbara which occurred sometime after Namadbara's experience with Yumbarrbarr and the tree. It is said to have happened somewhere near Mangulwan, in an 'open place'. Namadbara is sitting by himself, alone, thinking. Bill tells the story in Namadbara's words:

I was lying down. I listen. Noise.[39] I wake up. I bin wake up, listen. What this? That two short man, my friend — they made me friend — they bin come down [Namadbara's two spirit-helpers]. They said, 'We got to go.'

'Where?'

They bin just fly, I dunno. I dunno where we bin fly. I sit down three people, I dunno, one minute we was there. Big corroboree — devil [namarnde].

I was sitting down quiet, but that two kid, they were telling me, 'Quiet! You look that man, he's dead. He's dead orright, but he's going to wake.'

I bin get heart-crack [extreme fright]. That man bin dead, sleep, orright, bin wake now. And this man ['devil' namarnde], you know, bin come and cut im right off, his head.

I bin look up and I saw. Oh Christ! I bin shake like fuckin' hell! I bin frightened [of] that namarnde.

Namadbara's father, Marrarna, now appears.

M: 'You all right, son?'

N: 'Yeah, I'm all right — I dunno.'

M: 'What are you doing here?'

N: 'I dunno how come I came here.'

M: 'Yeah. You all right,' he said.

N: 'I went 'long big corroboree,' and [Namadbara told his father about it].

M: 'Son, come on! We go now.'

N: 'What I do, Daddy?' he bin ask im.

M: 'No worry. You sleep.'

N: 'Yeah, all right.'

M: 'I go home.'

N: 'Where?'

M: 'Mangulwan' [the ancestral Alardju clan site to which the spirit of an Alardju clan member returns upon death].

N: 'I come?'

M: 'No, you working buffalo.'

Bill: We bin there now, buffalo skin [work].

Later in his account, Bill adds some further details of the interaction between Namadbara and his father. Bill asks Namadbara what happened after the frightening incident:

Oh, your grandfa [Marrarna] bin come. 'Get up, son,' he said. 'Get up.'

I bin try get up.

M: 'Get up! Straighten em your leg,' him bin tell em, growlem.

Namadbara stood up, straightening his legs.

M: 'Hold strong.'

N: 'Daddy, where you going?'

M: 'Paddy, where you?'

But he [Namadbara] didn't answer. '[Marrarna] was gone.'

Namadbara's reputation

In assessing a marrkidjbu's reputation, Western Arnhem Landers come to characterise that person in terms of the amount or strength of their power. A number of marrkidjbu practitioners have been considered to have had 'only a little power' during their years of practice (see Berndt & Berndt 1970:145), or to have been able to demonstrate 'power' only in particular activities, such as song or dance. At the outset of Namadbara's career — after his first encounter with power — he was clearly ranked, as Jacob Nayinggul put it, as an 'ordinary' marrkidjbu with abilities and skills limited to simple healing. Namadbara himself told of an event in which he was involved with a number of others during a canoe sea journey, when Joe Cooper was still running the timber mills. In this he positions himself as a 'junior' ranking or 'novice' marrkidjbu behind an older, more experienced and skilled practitioner. At the time, according to the account of Thompson Yuludjiri, he was a 'young fella' and 'only a little bit clever'. 'He never bin come up to clever yet — only a little bit.'

However, over the years Namadbara was considered to have acquired stronger powers and was able to demonstrate a wide variety of 'clever' phenomena. Each person who spoke about Namadbara had a particular event in their memories of their life that for them was typical or indicative of his convincing power as a marrkidjbu. These ranged from small personal incidents or particular significant interactions of that person with Namadbara, to demonstrations and displays of his power at a public level.

In speaking of 'the margidjbu, or 'powerful man' in a 1951 paper, the Berndts (Berndt & Berndt 1951:76) expressed the opinion that 'much of his reputation appears to have been founded, ultimately, on his own accounts of his experiences,' after which they add the rider, 'although success or failure in "healing" is also an important factor'. In considering Namadbara's reported activities, it might rather be said the other way around — success or failure in healing (and other marrkidjbu activities) is the crucial factor in a marrkidjbu's reputation and a marrkidjbu's own accounts of their experiences are considered by others as simply confirmatory. There is a natural basis of scepticism in the community and clearly some contenders to this 'power' do not make the grade; others are able to maintain it, and their reputations grow with each perceived successful demonstration. As in other cultures and areas, whether the practitioner be considered a shaman, medicine man or a spirit medium, a clever person's claim to 'cleverness' is not accepted simply on the strength of his or her own proclamations. A marrkidjbu builds his or her reputation over the years, through demonstrations that eventually convince a majority of others of their abilities.[40] This process can be seen in Namadbara's career and his progressive development of a reputation, eventually as a marrkidjbu of great power and wisdom.

Kumula and the Wider Community

Dreams and visions

Through the 1940s and into the 1950s while Namadbara spent significant periods of time at Gunbalanya,[41] he increasingly focused on the collective as much as on the individual. Jacob Nayinggul describes how he would send out a message, call a meeting together and address the people, making prognostications about the future according to the dreams that he'd had. These are said to have always been related to what was happening in the real life of the community. In Jacob's words:

> Then, after everybody dancing, everybody happy, right. Everybody sitting down having a spell. Then he told people what's going on, how he felt, what sort of dream he had, because all his dreams — nearly — was connected to what was going on — life.

> And he could work it out from that dream.

One of the visions he had at this time related to the future of Iwaidja land on the Cobourg Peninsula, including his own mother's Country. In 1960, he sent a message to the Cooper family in Darwin, where they had moved after the death of their father, Reuben, that they should come and fight for their land — otherwise, 'the white fellas will take it all'. Cooper family members were a part of Namadbara's mother's Murran clan. Ron Cooper tells the story:

> He sent us a message-stick right to my mother — which she lost in the cyclone [Cyclone Tracy, 1974]: 'Tell my mother (my mother was his 'aunty') to unite us all and come and get together.'

Because he had a vision. And he said in his vision himself, he said, 'If you don't come and fight for your land, the white fella will come and take it.'

Which is what we naturally did. [But] we get Cobourg Peninsula [on a] 99-year lease. So we got to — every time we want to go somewhere or do something we got to go and ask the Board — of Conservation — if we can do something.[42]

He already said that. He knew!

IAN: So, it was a long time before the story about land-rights and everything came in? [Land rights legislation, the Aboriginal Land Rights (NT) Act, *was not introduced until 1976].*

He told my mother, 'Tell my cousin [Ron] to come back and claim for this land because at this stage, it's going to be their land. If they don't do it, they're going to lose it.'

At a more personal level, he assisted the people of his community at critical times in their lives. He would size up their situation and assist without his help necessarily being directly sought. Johnny Williams Snr (in the following paraphrased account) tells of some special help that he received from Namadbara in the early 1950s:

At the time John was about to go off to the Korean War. He went out to Cape Don on Cobourg Peninsula to visit his mum before he left. He was dressed in his new soldier's uniform and quite proud to show it off. But his mum was very upset to see him going off to war. She was crying, and he felt himself that it was likely he might not return. Old Paddy was camping there too. He told her that she didn't have to worry because her son would come back. In fact, he reassured her, her son would end up not going.

He took John aside, picked up a little flat stone from the ground, rubbed it under his armpit and gave it to him. He told him that when he goes back to Darwin to go to 'the colonel' and ask him for a discharge. 'Now, normally,' said John, 'you don't just walk up to the colonel and ask for a discharge, because you just won't get it.' However, Paddy told him to hold the little stone under his tongue while talking to the colonel and he would give him his discharge. A day or so later, he was back in Darwin and went up to the colonel at the Larrakeyah Barracks with the stone in his mouth and asked him for a discharge. To John's great surprise, the colonel said, 'OK. If you can get a government job, we'll dismiss you.' So the very next day he went to an acquaintance of his, who was a works supervisor at the Public Works Department. 'You can start next week,' he was told. He then took his 'start up' papers back to the colonel, who immediately wrote out his discharge. And he went on to work for the government department for the next 36 years.

'Marrkidjbu — but stronger and something else'

It was around the mid-to-late 1950s that Namadbara devised a ritual involving the whole community that centred on the wooden 'radio' with its empowering kunbalem, taken from the speared cat. At the time he was living in a small, brown wooden house in the section of Gunbalanya known as Banyan and it was here that he first carried it out. One night he invited all the Banyan people to come to a meeting outside his house. They danced first and then, while they were resting, he told them what he wanted them to do. Jacob Nayinggul tells the story:

And there in his room, in his house, he had this 'radio' kundulk. And he told people — he had a little fire going kumekbe kore kunrurrk, in that house. He had a little fire and two wires burning, like hot, to melt that kunbalem in that wood.

So, everybody who came — I was a sort of a worker for him — he told Bininj — everyone, Daluk and Bininj [women and men], one by one, to go into that room and he told them what to do. 'Pick up this wire, and when you put that wire kore [into] that radio, that hole, to melt that fat or to burn it, you also talk. Say what you want for this Gunbalanya. Just say what you want.'

Most of the people said, 'Ngadjare kunrurrk — I want house — more better — njamed [whatsaname] — conditions, more better treatment from missionary, from Balanda.'

[And then when one person had finished] she went out, or he, and another one came in — same thing. But everybody went for — njamed — better conditions.

Soon after this, when the Old Man was ready, he sent word around that everybody should come together again for a further meeting:

So he told others — that Nabulanj and Ngalkodjok, they're traditional owners [of the Gunbalanya area] — to let know people to get message across there, big camp other side [of Gunbalanya], to all come down here for that night — one night.

They all came down. All came down, where everybody had corroboree, dance. And then he made a speech — big talk. He told story about what's going to happen now, and that 'power'.

He told people that [it] will work on this Country — to make it a better town.

And everybody went, 'Yoh!' [Yes].

Following this, the wooden object, the kundulk with the empowered kunbalem, was put into an empty flour drum and buried in a specially dug hole in the Banyan area:

And all that word [kunwok] from all different people — [it was] built up into one [in the radio].

[But Namadbara warned everybody not to expect the things they had asked for to happen immediately].

But he said, '[It will take] a long time. But you [will] see it happen.'

The power in the drum was, even years later, considered potent. In 1995, when Jacob Nayinggul recounted this event, there were further new houses being built at Banyan. Jacob pointed to the drum site and said that he had just visited the Council office to ensure that the planned siting of houses would avoid the drum site itself.

In recounting the story about these rituals, people tell how there were no decent houses before this. But since the burial of the drums with Namadbara's 'power', houses have been built all around the vicinity, exactly as Namadbara predicted. Thompson Yuludjiri comments:

He buried might be four or five or, might be six drum he buried here — to that Banyan tree.

He told us [predicted] before all this house set in now.

That['s] his power [in the drum], his dreaming.

I don't know what. But he told us before all these houses build up. Now, we bin wait for a long time — for all these houses now, and the shop.

Bluey Ilkgirr and his wife Susan (Ngalkangila) also viewed this as a considerable personal achievement by Namadbara through his special power:

SI: Plenty houses longa Oenpelli. Him bin clever man, im bin put something there. In the drum there im bin put something. You seen them houses there, Oenpelli?

BI: Gunbalanya! All that houses! No bin houses before! But when that Old Man him bin finish [carrying out the rituals], and his brother [Wilambilam] too — and [now] they bin makem [houses] all over the place.

The ritual was repeated in other places. A drum with a similarly empowered object was buried in the Arrkuluk area of Gunbalanya, and Namadbara also carried out the ritual at Minjilang. People at Minjilang point out the place where the drum is buried — by some houses in the middle of the town. It is a place that is not to be disturbed, with pandanus trees now growing all around. It is said that the fat is leaking out slowly so that the power gets evenly distributed for the regulated and controlled development of Minjilang. If the drum were to be disturbed, the development of the community might go awry.

Namadbara also carried out a slightly different procedure at Gunbalanya, but again involving drums buried at specific sites. Again the drums contained all the words of the people — Jacob Nayinggul explains that, in this instance, they were words written on paper rather than spoken.

He did it another way too.

He made them have djura [pieces of paper].

They got djura. And when they talk, he had people writing — simple. They just went like this [demonstrates 'running writing' on paper]:

eeeeeeeeeeeeee   aaaaaaaaaaaa   ooooooooooooo

And while [the person] was doing like this, that person had to talk.

And [JN emphasised], all this had meaning.

As with the other procedure, they had to say what they wanted for the future of Gunbalanya, or for their own individual aspirations. All the papers on which the 'words' were written were then put into a drum and ceremonially buried. Jacob says that his mother, for instance, became the first Aboriginal community nurse in Gunbalanya through this procedure, involving Namadbara's empowering kumula. She, in turn, went on to train others in nursing skills. Jacob himself performed this 'writing' procedure, under Namadbara's instructions. He asked to become a stockman and went on to succeed in this enterprise, though abandoned this pursuit after an accident.

Bluey Ilkgirr witnessed the burying of such a drum with papers inside it. The present location of the Gunbalanya Health Clinic is considered to be due to Namadbara's prior burial of a drum at this site containing such 'words' (aspirations) of the people. He is said to have foreseen through vision this site as being the site for a 'hospital':

You know the hospital — Clinic?

They bin put it, big box, a sort of drum — and all the paper. A lot of paper — might be over a million. And they bin do it theirself, and all that word.

Not proper writing like this [pointing to a book] — just ordinary [handwriting].

It was to this community scale or level of functioning that Jacob alludes when he describes Namadbara as having achieved 'a new level, a higher level of operation' as a marrkidjbu. Namadbara continually sought to engage the community in coming to terms with its potential role of shaping its own future, despite the outlook being one increasingly dominated by Balanda processes. Clearly, the drum empowerment procedures were a part of this community engagement. Jacob Nayinggul stated:

First, nobody did that before — before him.

Every main traditional owner [even] he didn't know that idea.

[Namadbara] was the only one who came up with that idea — that power. Like marrkidjbu — [but] not that marrkidjbu that makes you better [not the healing side of marrkidjbu business] — but this one, another [side of] marrkidjbu. Yeah, marrkidjbu but different way. [This was] stronger, and something else.

This series of rituals can clearly be seen as an attempt on the part of Namadbara to wrest some of the control of the situation at Oenpelli back into the hands of the Aboriginal residents, to empower them to realise that they could have some control over their future, rather than let them feel like helpless pawns of mission and government policy.

Making leaders for the community

As an empowering marrkidjbu — that is, through giving kumula or 'purpose for that job' — Namadbara sought to make leaders in the community. As Jacob puts it, 'Bininj being boss for Bininj people' — leaders who would not be overwhelmed by the mission Balanda. Jacob tells of observing Namadbara one day using his 'writing method' to do this:

And he had made himself three or four pages, like a book.

He sat down and I watched him [talking] when he was doing it:

'And make me leaders for this community . . .'

Jacob went on to name a number of Gunbalanya people who were elevated into leadership roles in the community, with assistance from Namadbara's empowering kumula. Likewise, at Minjilang it is acknowledged that Namadbara made leaders through such empowerment, and two of the leading women there consider that Namadbara's 'help' gave them the impetus to develop into their present leading community roles.

People also gained faith in Namadbara's powers through the success of rituals he devised and performed at the more public level, such as the drum burying rituals. People point to all the houses that have since been built as a result of Namadbara's power in the buried drums.

In recounting the story of the drum rituals that Namadbara had devised and undertaken, Jacob Nayinggul also recounted an incident that occurred sometime in the later 1950s, as an illustration of the sort of power that Namadbara was able to wield and the respect his authority was held in among the Gunbalanya

Namadbara (third from left), in his role as leader and overseeing guide for an 'expedition' to Mt Borradaile, in the context of establishing the First Aboriginal Mining Company (FAMCO), 1971. Photo: George Chaloupka.

community residents. Thompson Yuludjiri also commented on the same incident. Apparently an argument of some nature had occurred between Wilambilam and Namadbara which ended up with Wilambilam digging up one of Namadbara's drums. 'He tipped out the drum and let all the power escape.' Namadbara 'was very unhappy' and the outcome was that he 'punished' the whole community by 'stopping' tobacco for a long period — Jacob remembered the ban lasting about nine months. He remembers helping his mother scratching around on the ground collecting old cigarette butts, 'Everybody was starving — for baccy!' Some people remember having to go to Mudginberri, others as far as Pine Creek (some 250 kilometres and many days' walk away) to get tobacco. Jacob commented, 'That was the strongest punishment he had.' And then he added, reflecting on the present Gunbalanya community, 'We should have that kind of power to stop beer!'

The anthropologist Catherine Berndt provides a further example of the power of both Namadbara and Wilambilam, on public display at Gunbalanya, providing reassurance and certainty at a time of crisis:

. . . people were eagerly awaiting the arrival of wet season stores for the mission . . . Stormy weather and repairs to the barge concerned had several times delayed its departure from Darwin, and rumours were rife about when it could be expected. European foods . . . were almost finished [and people] were 'starving' for tobacco . . . In addition, the low-lying ground around the Oenpelli billabong had been flooding after heavy rains, and the [water table] had been rising so that some of the new tin huts in the camp had toppled aslant. In this time of speculation and crisis, Namadbara and Wilambilam called people together for a series of ceremonies. Wilambilam had seen in a dream, he said, his spirit familiars, which had told him to summon everyone so that their friend, the 'frog that died', could come to life again. He was speaking about a spirit familiar or spirit child of Namadbara, sometimes identified with a secret-sacred object, believed to be buried under the ground. 'This frog is a margidjbu [marrkidjbu], he wants to live again. Come and share in this end-of-mourning feast, let us "work" together in this rite . . . ' People assembled at the ceremonial ground or 'ring place'. In the course of the ceremony, a dream-message was conveyed to them from the two spirit familiars . . . 'Don't worry', was the gist of this message. 'Everything will be all right. We didn't let those houses fall over for nothing [It was a sign]. The boat with the stores couldn't come before because of the frog that died. We buried him, and now we have revived him through this ceremony, and all will be well. Don't be anxious, the boat will come soon. Perhaps the day after tomorrow you will hear word of it. It is on its way and everything will be all right . . . ' 'We believe those two margidjbu,' several [of the people] said. 'They always know, those spirits tell them in dreams . . . ' It so happened that several days after the last ceremony word came that the barge had in fact left Darwin at last (Berndt 1964: 276–277).[43]

Controlling the power of Ngalyod, the Rainbow Serpent

Ngalyod, glossed in English by Aboriginal people today as the Rainbow Serpent, is both the fundamental creative expression of continuing life and, at the same time, its original initiator, the bringer of life to Western Arnhem Land — the 'First Mother' (see Berndt & Berndt 1970; Taylor 1987:266–275). The concept of Ngalyod is, however, also tied up in some way with the clever person's ability to wield power (mankordang/marrngkidj) (Spencer 1914:292–296; Berndt & Berndt 1992:233, 251). The power of a ngalyod is available to those clever enough to be able to harness or control it. Some clever people are said to have or to possess a ngalyod (ngalyod kakarrme) — usually considered to be located in their stomach region. This possession of ngalyod is what is said to make them clever.[44] Like other 'power objects' within the body (as described earlier), the ngalyod is also vulnerable. It can be lost. Among several contemporary Western Arnhem Landers who are said to have once possessed Ngalyod, it is now said to have been lost, or left and gone away — for a variety of reasons. Ngalyod can be sent out of the body on missions to magically penetrate other people, for harm or for other purposes. Perhaps more usually, they can be drawn out of bodies of water where they usually reside to be used for the purposes of the clever person.

Namadbara, in Jacob's account of the revival of the 'dead' cat, is said to have drawn the ngalyod (or the 'power' of the ngalyod) out of the nearby river in the form of the whirlwind, which then empowered the cat's revival. Clearly, it is a power that is very potent — it will be recalled that Jacob had to protect his own genitals from its power as it swept past him.

Husband and wife Bluey and Susan Ilkgirr tell of quite a different demonstration performed by Namadbara in front of a large group of people one night at Gunbalanya at a place near the present site of the Social Club. For this performance, Namadbara enlisted the aid of Bluey and several other men. On this occasion, Namadbara revealed the power he had to manipulate Ngalyod. He was demonstrating on his wife, Ngalkangila. It would seem from the following account that he was attempting to 'make her clever' — give her some 'power' — although the manki manki[45] object mentioned is usually associated with sorcery activity. He 'kills' her (makes her unconscious), then revives her again:

BI: That old lady, Ngalkangila — im [Namadbara] bin try to makem that girl [turn her into a clever woman]. But too hard.

SI: Im bin kill im all right. Im might be [made unconscious/'killed' as a precursor to being made clever].

BI: Kill im dead!

SI: Im bin kill im.

BI: We bin watchim 'bout [everybody was looking on]. And im bin kill im dead. That [Ngalkangila]. Im bin die!

Now we bin kill im, this one now.

If we 'make' im, [then it will be] orright [The onlookers and assistants were distressed and anxious that she may not be revived].

SI: Orright, im bin kill im now. Longa foot, im bin kill im. Ahh! Im bin look.

'No more cry!' im bin talk [to] whole lot [of us].

'You fella no more cry! Leave im lying dead.'

BI: Orright, we said, we believe. We bin believe, whole lot [of us]. Me, two, three, my brother, and myself. That's all we bin go — four people, and himself, that 'clever man'.

SI: Everybody bin look — kill im.

BI: And he said, 'We gonna kill im this girl.'

'Oh no! You gonna kill im?' we said.

SI: 'You fella look!' [says Namadbara].

BI: That ngalyod, im bin kill im long time, but im [Ngalkangila] no bin move. Big one! [the ngalyod].

No move — just little bit.

Im bin tellem me, little bit. 'You come out little bit, you get im,' [instructs Namadbara].

SI: Orright, all bin watchiiiiing.

BI: We bin looking im there. Im bin move [Ngalkangila].

SI: Im bin move, move.

BI: Hey! Im bin get up now all right. Hey! Im bin get up now, im proper woman now!

Talk talk now: 'Hey, whattim, I bin die?'

'You're all right. Just go home,' [Namadbara instructs her].

We bin takem [her] home too.

SI: But that one girl [Ngalkangila], im bin takem that way, Ngalyod.

Now, he bin kill im, this side, longa milkwood tree, near that Club [in explanation of where the event took place].

BI: Big mob, we bin camp there.

IAN: And what did Nabulanj do to make that Ngalkangila get up?

BI: Im bin do something there. Im bin makem like that [demonstrates drawing a circle with his foot], like that — little one.

IAN: Circle, eh?

BI: Yeah. Circle im bin makem. Orright. Im bin clearem that ground. Orright, im bin makem that circle. Orright, im bin come out there, that girl now — he [Ngalyod] bin spew. Spew. Vomit.

IAN: Vomit? Webmeng?

BI: Yeah, webmeng. That ngalyod webmeng, nabiwebmen im there that girl [the Rainbow vomited up Namadbara's wife].

SI: Im little baby like, that girl, im wife now.[46]

BI: They savvy. Everybody they savvy — that Old Man.

And we bin look that ngalyod, im bin have im longa hand, eh? Sort of a needle.

SI: Manki manki.

BI: Manki manki it's called.

SI and BI: Manki manki — longa Ngalyod. [On a later occasion BI explained that the manki manki came out of the mouth of the ngalyod].

BI: Just pullim out one [manki manki]. Yeah. Im bin just pull im out one. Well, im bin just go and put im there, longa — buried. Right, put im there. Orright, we bin look again. Im bin come out [of] that ngalyod. Im bin like that [demonstrates — putting out tongue].

Yes, im bin makem finish.

SI: We fella bin look — [the manki manki was a] black one too.

BI: All that black one — spots.

SI: All the manki manki, im bin turn up here.

IAN: And this was at night-time, kukak?

SI: Kukak [night-time] that time he bin killim longa im wife.

For those present, this was clearly an impressive display of Namadbara's powers and an event which has stayed in the forefront of Bluey and Susan's memories of Namadbara. Bluey concluded his account clearly considering that this episode demonstrated beyond doubt Namadbara's pre-eminence as a clever man:

Hey! Too clever! Proper, proper clever man!

Some months after this account was first given, I went back and questioned Bluey and Susan again — trying to clarify in my own mind what had 'really' taken place during this event. In this I was unsuccessful. Nevertheless, although unable to assist the reader with a more comprehensible rendition of the story, I have retained it not only on account of the event's significance to the witnesses, but the fact that similar events have been recorded elsewhere in Aboriginal Australia. Bluey explained that the ngalyod had licked Ngalkangila and that there were red meat ants (djak) crawling all over her body, but they were not ordinary ants but 'big ones belong[ing] to Ngalyod'. The ngalyod swallowed her 'biwukmeng' — then vomited her out. The manki manki came out of the mouth of the ngalyod. They added the detail that white manki manki were 'no good'; that a yellow manki manki was a 'good one'. [I did not ask them to comment on what black ones with spots meant]. It was a moonlit night.

Namadbara was considered too clever to be defeated even by the ngalyod power of an evil-intentioned adversary. On one occasion that Namadbara told Thompson and other Gunbalanya people about, someone with the power to project their ngalyod and use it for harmful purposes tried to kill Namadbara. However, Namadbara demonstrated that he had superior power by successfully repelling the attack, again demonstrating his control over Ngalyod — a considerable achievement — and thereby enhancing his status as a practitioner of superior qualities. He told Thompson Yuludjiri that his two spirit-helpers forewarned him, so that they could go out and confront and defeat the ngalyod. The next day, he described to everybody what had happened to him:

One time that Nabulanj told me that they bin 'singing' this Rainbow Serpent [conjuring up the Rainbow Serpent through the use of chants], com[ing] from down that way [southeast], come to kill that Old Man.

That ngalyod bin come half-way, and these two young fella [spirit-helpers] bin tellim: 'Yoh, that ngalyod gonna come up and kill you. More better we go back, see that ngalyod.'

They went there. They see that ngalyod coming — might be they bin killim, or what? [Anyway, they] stop im — couldn't come any more here, this way. They bin stop im, finish.

Next day, he bin telling me — not only me, but everyone — [told] us story. I don't know why [they tried to kill him]. Might be they bin think they gonna 'sing' that clever man, him send im this ngalyod here to killim. [But] that Nabulanj bin know that ngalyod.

Passing on the Power

Namadbara's 'power objects'

Something of the nature of Namadbara's powers is revealed in conversations that Bill Neidjie reconstructs and reproduces from those that he had with Namadbara over the years. Like practitioners of clever business in many other parts of Australia,[47] the special power(s) that Namadbara had was conceived as being embodied in a 'power object' located in each of two different parts of his body. In the area at the back of his neck or upper back, he held the power that he had acquired during the sugarbag experience, in the form of a longish and hard piece of kubbulak mankung (the kubbulak variety of sugarbag). The second object, in his stomach area, was a small round stone about the size (as it was explained to me) of the tip of a cigarette. No account was given as to whether this last object related to any particular experience of Namadbara's.

Little is said of how Namadbara may have actually used or manipulated the power objects in his marrkidjbu practice during his life. However, their significance as objects of power become clearer in his instructions to some of those close to him as he approached his death. He urged them to be present as he died so that the power might 'jump out' and into the nearby person, who would thereby receive the power and become clever — be transformed. In Big Bill's account, the Old Man tells him when he knows that it won't be long, 'close up finish':

Gettin' weak. So, if he jump out, you might sit alongside, he might jump to you. This power will come to you. If you long way, you gonna miss.

You come beside me — you hang on me — something might get in your body.

However, Bill was elsewhere at the time of Namadbara's passing. The message came 'two days late' and he missed the opportunity for this gift of power — a matter about which he continues to feel regret. But, he says, some young men who were there,

'They said he was melt, you know — like matches — he [the power] was jump out [of] his body.'[48]

Bluey Ilkgirr's account also presents a similar conception, although a slightly different understanding of the power objects inherent in Namadbara's body. Namadbara instructed them:

'When I die, you fellas take em out here [pointing to stomach]. Then you fellas clever. No more fright!' [Don't be frightened to do it].

But we bin sorry longa that Old Man. Ohh! We can't do that! We can't cut im and take em out that thing, little one, stone.

Well, he bin havem that one. [If] we [had] tried to take [it] out, we'd bin gonna all [become] clever.

But we bin thinkin' about — ohh, we can't do — we bin tellim that Old Man.

[But he said] 'You can take em out. You people got to take em out. When I bin growem up you mob.[49] Don't frighten! [After all, I've been your advisor all your lives, so trust me now].

'Soon as when I die, then take em out. Two, one on the back and one here.'

But we [couldn't] do it. We sorry like — because like a father. Im growem up we.

This clever power, mankordang/marrngkidj, then, can 'jump out' of a body — not only at death but at any time during one's life.[50] It is thus vulnerable and a person has to be careful not to lose it. It can disappear, never to return. From all the accounts, this did not happen to Namadbara who seemed to guard against this possibility. He was very careful with his power. He was careful to never touch alcohol. Big Bill has him saying:

'No drink grog, maybe kill im [power]. Im jump out. If anyone good [a likely candidate], they should leavem drink [or] power might go away.'

But that Old Man, he never touch anything. They used to bringem long Timber Mill some rum and whiskey.

'Old Man, do you want any?'

He said, 'Nah. I don't like it. If I take that one, I might lose my power.'

Neither would he cut or allow others to cut his fingernails. Several of those who give accounts of the Old Man have remarked particularly on how long his fingernails were. James Wauchope looked after Namadbara in his later years and said, 'They were like talons, they were curved around and about four inches long. I used to have to light a cigarette for him. His fingernails were too long to handle a match. "Come on, I'll cut your fingernails, Old Man." But he wouldn't let me.' Something of his power was tied up in his uncut fingernails. In Bill Neidjie's words:

He never cuttim fingernail. Fingernail, he was long. He bin leave em. We said [to Namadbara], 'Might cuttim. No good, you know, fingernail like this.'

'No good cuttim, leave em. If you cut this fingernail [then] whole lot something be happen [to you all].'

[Namadbara didn't] want to spoil [harm] people. He don't want to killim people.

'I don't want to kill em. But you mob cut this one here [then] you doing it [you would be doing harm to yourselves].'

So that Old Man, properly marrkidjbu, I believe.

'He gave me this gift'

Although no candidate was successful in directly taking on his mantle of powers, different individuals are credited with having received a certain aspect of power from Namadbara. To some, it was the power to succeed in their chosen enterprises (kumula), for others it was the power necessary to take on community leadership, and on others he bestowed the gift, albeit temporary, of 'psychic' abilities.

Ron Cooper (Mulurinj) names Namadbara as one of the four men who were his principal teachers before the Second World War, when he was growing up on Cobourg Peninsula at his father's timber mill camps. Ron was then 'going through the rules' — attending the major Ubarr (Wuwalk) ceremonies:

He taught many things to many people.

He showed me how to leave my body and go somewhere else, to see what other people are doing and to come back. I could lay at night [in Darwin], and go to Arnhem Land. He could read your mind — who you are, where you came from.

But this man already gave me this gift. I could understand everybody else.

You know, like my wife, she used to get really wild with me, 'What are you looking at the people for?' He showed me — I could read people's mind. 'What are you looking at that person for?' And she'd get jealous, because I could read a person's mind.

You know, he could go — say, for instance, we had a place to go to, say we were going from Gameragi [Black Point area, Cobourg Peninsula] to Wamanyi [Cape

Brogden area], or somewhere else, he would name a tree, and say that this is the tree we're going to look for [describe the specific tree], this is the tree where we going. We could be 50 miles away, but we ended up in front of that tree — how many forks, how many branches it would have on this tree. Now, how would he know that? And my mother called him 'Compass' [because] he could go and take you there, direct — 'this is the place we're looking for.'

IAN: So how do you think he knew that? Because he could see it [in his mind's eye]?

Yeah. He could see it before he went there. His body, his spirit — would go there and have a look at it and come back and tell us where it was. Don't you forget — a wonderful gift he had, you know.

IAN: You said that he showed you how to leave your body and go somewhere else?

Well, that's right.

IAN: And did he just — gave you that power, or did he instruct you?

No, he blessed me, and gave me his power. If you want to go and see someone, and if there is an urgent reason, or you want to go and look if the family is all right, then the power was given to me. And — that was a beautiful power.

He gave me this gift, but when he died, he took this gift from me because I didn't fulfil my duty, my promise — to see him [at the time that he was dying]. I lost this gift which he gave me, this beautiful gift.

You know, I could travel to Adelaide, to wherever I wanted to go. Once I was at Cape Don, and I wanted to check on my family [in Darwin]. And I flew back — at night, and I seen the house. Where's my missus? Oh, she was at a party. And I went and seen that. She was at this party, and I named the people [who were there]. When I came back, I told her. 'How you did that?' [she wanted to know]. But I went there![51]

You see, this was something that Old Man taught me. But I've lost it.

IAN: And you were able to tell your wife, the other people who were at that party?

Yeah. Everyone. She got the shock of her life. I could name everyone in the place.

IAN: And were you, like, asleep? When you went on this, this travel?

I was at Cape Don. The body — this — you just leave. You could see yourself. You get up and — shit!

IAN: Oh, you could look down and see yourself down there on the ground?

Yes. But it was a gift — was given by this man. And maybe, when he died, withered away.

'This power, too hard'

Over the years there were a few men who approached Namadbara and asked him to pass his power on to them, to 'give it' to them. Namadbara did, but it appears his power proved 'too strong' for them so that these aspiring 'clever blokes' were ultimately unsuccessful in fully acquiring the power. Namadbara also tried to transmit his power to his son, in this case unbidden, but his son backed fearfully away from it, finding it 'just too frightening'. The accounts speak of very frightened men, some running away.[52] In one case, a search party went out looking for the man.

Clearly, there was a great barrier of fear to overcome by anyone wishing to follow this route to gaining mankordang. Facing one's fear and eventually overcoming it was something that had to be endured — a necessary prerequisite in ultimately achieving mastery of the power. Namadbara told Thompson Yuludjiri that it took a long time to gradually become accustomed to the power and for the fear to eventually subside: 'That power — five or six years to make you quiet'.

A Gunbalanya songman (a singer, considered to have some power to 'dream' new songs) who had stopped to listen to Thompson's description of men running away in fear, agreed and said that anybody who wanted to make a 'friend' of the namarnde ('devils', such as the two 'children' of Namadbara) had to face their fear. 'After two or three years it goes away,' he said.

Towards the end of his life, without any apparent successes in passing on his power, Namadbara (according to Bill Neidjie's account) clearly felt that it was just too difficult for the majority of people to take on. Bill has him saying:

'Yeah, too hard. Too hard orright.

I oughta teach you [Bill] long time ago when we bin [were at] Mangulwan. Now too late' [He does not have the strength necessary to pass on the power].

He said, 'I woulda bin, you know, eight years' time [to teach you], I woulda take you bush, leave you there and you woulda gettim [power] proper then.[53]

'But now I'm too old. I can't do anything now. Very weak.

I gave two bloke my power [at Cape Don, Cobourg Peninsula].

[Those] two I gave em power, really power. And that two man, they never sleep anything, no [too frightened to sleep].

Maybe they bin get heart-crack [extreme fright]. I don't know.

They bin run away. Might be something — power too strong, might be.'

Clearly, one had to have a predisposition for this acquisition of power, or the strength of character to persevere:

'Me, the last one now [last marrkidjbu] — finish. What you wanna do?' [Namadbara asked Bill].

I said, 'I don't know, I can't do anything [clever]. Nothing. I don't know much [about] what kind power you got.'

He said, '[It's] very strong.'

Namadbara then gives Bill an account of his attempt to instruct the two frightened candidates:

He said, 'We bin sitting down there [at] Cape Don [when] I made that two' [gave or showed them power — mankordang].

Anyhow, they bin sitting down there, [becoming] dark. And he said, 'No, we sit down yet.' Another hour, they bin sit down another hour.

This man [Yumbarrbarr], he come out.

Old Man said, 'Don't move, he [won't] kill us.'

[But] this mob they bin shuttem up eye. They bin frightened!

And the Old Man, he said, 'Go on, you fella, open up you fella eye. Look!'

Nah. They bin shuttem up eye.

[After this event he instructed them] 'Look, when we come out home, you mob sleep. Don't tell any story — anything again. If you tell em story [tell others about what happened], you gotta be fright yourself [make yourselves frightened]. You know? But no more tell em story [and] you'll be all right. But if you tell em story — you can tell em story, but you'll be frightened one. When you see somebody, you'll run away. You know?'

But apparently they did tell some others what they had experienced and consequently re-evoked their terror, became very frightened and took off into the bush. One man made his way along the coast from Cape Don towards his home at Croker Island (he was not a young man — 'little bit grey hair'). He was gone for several days and Big Bill, along with a local Balanda, Dave Lindner, were among those involved in searching for him. They caught up with him at one stage, but while in their camp, the frightened man observed Dave oiling and cleaning his gun, and ran off again, imagining that they were trying to kill him. When he

On a visit to Namadbara's Country in 2003, his nephew Archie Brown performs mortuary ritual ochreing at Namadbara's old camp site at Mangulwan where his spirit resides. Photo: Murray Garde.

reached the mainland, opposite Croker, he found a floating kapok log and with its help, paddled and swam his way across. In his telling of the story, Bill later asked this man why he swam across:

'My eye was sleepy, and people ['spirits'?] they were talking to me.'

I said, 'What you frightened for?'

He said, 'Dangerous!'

On Croker, people asked him why he had swum across and he told them that people on the mainland were trying to kill him. 'But it wasn't true,' Thompson Yuludjiri commented. In his account of the incident, Thompson says that after this, the man would imagine whenever he saw a group of people sitting around at a camp talking and laughing that they were plotting to kill him — 'but really they were only [chatting]'.

Big Bill reports Namadbara as commenting afterwards:

'Well, I bin spoil em. They bin run. That thing I told you [about] [yumbarrbarr] bin come out. And they bin run away. Tryin to run away. They bin come out and tell em story [against Namadbara's direct instructions]. That's why they frighten. They shouldn't tell em story or keep it [should have kept it to themselves]. [Then] they woulda bin all right.'

Namadbara must have been upset at the outcome of the incident. He says to Bill:

'I gave them that power from me. And they frightened [of] everything. They gonna get me now.'

Thompson Yuludjiri also tells of another man who had tried an apprenticeship with Namadbara, but likewise had ended up too frightened by the whole thing. One day he and this man were motoring in their boat down Bowen Strait, between Croker and the mainland, when they saw a dark, overarching and threatening wet season storm coming — not an unusual event at that time of year. Thompson was all for simply maintaining their direct course and motoring straight through it, but the other man became extremely fearful and agitated and insisted that they make straight for the shore. From there on they hugged the shoreline until they reached their destination. Thompson said that he realised that it was 'the Old Man's power' that had made his companion so very frightened.

The account by Namadbara's son, Robert Djorlom, provides further insight into the nature of the fearful mental events that need to be endured if control of the power is to be acquired:

One night, it was cold weather time, July. I was sleeping at Forestry — Murgenella, Wak — and suddenly I was dreaming about it, namarnde. And suddenly a shadow came up to me and, when I opened my eyes, I couldn't — I was — my mind was gone, you know? I couldn't hear anything, or feel it. So I run out through the door to Tim and old Joseph. And I told them, 'Hey! Tim, grab my arm!' And I told old Joseph too, 'You grab my other arm, and step on my foot, because — I don't know, I might fly [away].'

So they did. They stepped on my foot, and Tim thought, 'Maybe if I bite his ear so he can listen, feel it.'

So he bit my two ears, and I felt all my memory come back to me. And I realised then that I heard that bird, you know, that kurrwilluk [curlew].[54] He talked three times. And I said to them, 'Did you hear that?'

They said, 'Yeah.'

'That's the one now. It's after me!'

The next morning I went down to Wurrngki, where Henry was living — that old marrkidjbu. I told him, 'Maybe something wrong with me? Maybe they bin kill me? [Has someone used kunkidj (sorcery) against me?] Can you have a look at me?'

'Mah! [Ok]. Come here.'

And he took me, told me to stand up — towards the sun, and he was behind me, and he came running there, sniffing, you know, if he could smell any bad smell on me. But, nothing. And he pulled my hair, on this side — right-hand side, and left-hand side — and nothing happened. [If hair had come out in his hand it would have been an indicator that sorcery had been used and that Robert might soon die]. And stepped on my heel and the other heel.

And he said to me, 'Ah, nothing happening to you. Maybe your old man is testing you. Is trying to givem you power.'

IAN: And you were frightened?

Yeah! And then I went back to Murgenella, Wak. And then I thought that maybe it went away. So I slept another night. Then I slept another night. It happened again.

IAN: In the dream, or — reality?

Really, real! I could hear that bird and my heart was beating, and I got very scared.

So it took me a long time. I went to Croker Island and asked my Old Man. He was still at Croker. 'What's wrong, Dad? [Is] there something wrong with me? I always have a dream — aah, I mean not dream, but really — that bird come and talk to me, and then I feel frightened?'

But he just said to me, 'Maybe it's just happening to you. He like to make you [a] friend.'

And then I thought maybe this Old Man is keeping it secret. He don't want to tell me.

And then I went back again [to Murgenella] and worked there. But it was still happening. Then I thought, oh, maybe it's better for me to get away from here.

So I went to Oenpelli — left my job, told my boss, 'go for holiday'. He gave me six week[s]. And I went to Oenpelli and got another job, working at mining. Yeah. But it was still following me, that bird.

I left that job and went with another old fellow, Phillip Dirdi, to Mangulwan. And we stayed there, working on the airstrip. We stayed there one night, and she came again. And I could hear that kurrwilluk. And she was talking. Then I told old Phillip, 'Hey, give me gun, and I shoot that bird.'

He said, 'No, don't shoot that bird! If you shoot that bird, that bullet might turn around and shoot you!'

Then I gave it to him, that gun, and we went to Oenpelli.

Again I stayed there. Oh, maybe I get a bible, I thought. Then I read every page of that thing — scripture. And it started to fade away, little by little.

Then I thought, oh, maybe that one really work, and I'll go and have a beer.

I got really mad — drinking beer.

IAN: And did the drinking the beer . . . ?

No. Still the bird was [there].

And then I got married and moved here [Goulburn Island]. The bird was still following me. It followed me till — maybe [for] three or four years' time. Long time. And it stopped.

IAN: Just stopped suddenly or . . . just fade away?

Finish, fade away. It won't come again.

IAN: And did you ever ask your dad, Nabulanj, like tell him, 'Oh, I'm sick of this bird always calling — I don't want him'?

No. I just knew him — I knew this Old Man test me.

IAN: But, too frightening?

Too frightening. Yeah. 'Cause that one [was] when my Old Man still alive. But when he died then that bird went away.

Namadbara's nephew Archie Brown, linguist Nicholas Evans and archaeologist Kim Akerman pay their respects at Namadbara's grave, Mountnorris Bay, 2003. Photo: Murray Garde.

After these less than satisfactory experiences with trying to pass on his gift and towards the end of his life, Namadbara emphasised to Big Bill the difficulty of getting this power. Bill says that he regretted not having 'got' some of the power from Namadbara, and that Namadbara now admitted to him that he had 'made a mistake' with those he had tried to introduce to the power. They did not apply themselves consistently nor sufficiently to the task. 'I was wrong,' he told Bill. They had not been 'good enough'

'This one like it little bit, [then] walk off, come back little bit, listen, sit down, he walk off [again]. That not right,' he was telling me. 'They [are] not worth it,' he told me. 'They oughta bin get what I got — story [about power]. Woulda bin right [then] when I pass away. But that young fella, he gone mad. Yeah, they won't listen, anything. I tell em story [about power], they run away. They don't listen. Don't want to listen. No good they can't listen.'

'I [will] try this one [a candidate for power],' [says Namadbara to himself]. 'Too hard,' [says the candidate]. 'You get back into line and start again!' [Namadbara tells him]. Nothing.

To get the power, then, is very difficult, 'too hard'. In Big Bill's account, Namadbara is saying that you have to have a mind that is capable of maintaining an undistracted condition, of entering — in effect — a meditative state and that as soon as you become distracted, you lose it (the mental condition necessary for accessing the power). Persistence is required.[55] Bill recounts Namadbara's advice several times. On one occasion Namadbara tells Bill:

'If you quiet and go and sit down [by] yourself — no matter all day.

[If] you can't get it? [Then] go back again! Try [again].

Anything noise, you can't gettim. You know, you [have] got to go quiet [place], no more noise, anything. And no people walking around bush, or working somewhere — you [won't] gettim.

Hide in the bush. You can sit down by yourself.

If you makem one feeling [one mind], that's all — no more worry, anything. You might gettim then.

If quiet — you keep im one mind, [then] you gettim.

[But if] too many minds [then] you forget [become distracted].'

And I bin try sit down and think about, [but] too many mind yet, too many think [too much thinking, too many thoughts].

'You can't gettim,' he said, 'if you think about other way. [If] you got two, three, in your feeling, you know, mind — well, no good. If you makem one feeling

— that's all — think about it. If not, if you think about too much you can't get it — too hard.'[56]

Namadbara advised Bill that if he could keep his mind quiet, that 'tree he might pick you, and come. If you think about — tree will pick you up, telling you to come. But if you think about too many, you can't. Too hard.'

'And that tree has power,' says Namadbara — revealing further his relationship with the tree's power.

He said, 'That tree I can walk through. That tree he'll open up. If people, they run up [are chasing me], they might kill me, [then] I'll hide that tree. They won't kill me. I know that tree will help me. Well, tree he got power, I got power — but different [to] you mob. You don't gettim.'[57]

Nevertheless, he impressed on Bill the knowledge that trees (kundulk) 'might help him':

Well, one tree, he might be with you. He gotta explain to you. You can't listen. But that kundulk — this tree here, he'll be — might be — they'll help you.

Despite this lack of success in transmitting his power fully, there were other levels of awareness and sensitivity to the surrounding environment that Namadbara did bring out in several people, as revealed above.

His Death — and After

In his later life as he grew frailer, Namadbara frequented Gunbalanya less often and spent more and more time in small camps on the northwestern Arnhem coast and on Croker Island. He passed away on 12 August 1978 at his beach camp at Waliwanyun on Mountnorris Bay, just near the Wildji 'barge landing'. However, no candidate was present to 'pick up' his power as it left his dying body — although, according to the report that Bill Neidjie received, his power did 'jump out', 'melting — like matches'.[58] The traditional murlil mortuary rites were carried out and his body was finally buried in a sand dune behind the beach near Wildji. According to all accounts, an antbed (termite mound)[59] is growing out of his grave, a manifestation of his sacred power. This was something which should never be touched or damaged, reported Bluey Ilkgirr:

[They buried him] and im [the termite mound] bin shoot up that, njamed, black one — konjdja. That little antbed, that black antbed one.

Well, that spirit, im. Im bin shoot up, you know, that place where the graveyard. Danger. You can't go touching that one. Everybody wouldn't do that. We can't break it because otherwise we finished [harm would come to us]. Because he's too clever. Because he gottim kundjak [a form of sacred and dangerous power].[60] Him proper clever man that one.

As an accomplished marrkidjbu, Namadbara had necessarily gained control over his own 'spirit'[61] and had developed an ability to manipulate it during the course of his life. From this achieved understanding of his spirit he considered that, after his body had died, his spirit would nevertheless continue to have power to communicate with those in the world of the living. Before he died, Namadbara told Bill Neidjie:

'When I bin finish, don't put me 'long coffin. I don't want coffin. Where you leave me, you'll be leavem all the bone. But I'll be stand[ing] up watching you.'

IAN: *After he's finished?*

'When I finish,' [he] said, 'that spirit I'll ask — that bone and everything, my body be there, but I'll be standing, my spirit behind your back. I don't want to come out [become manifest], you might get heart-crack. You might get heart-crack and drop — unless you got heart. [Then] I'll come out. [But] if you fright . . . '

I said, 'I can't run away.'

He said, 'You might be all right, but nobody else, by yourself. I'll come out – tell you something.'

Big Bill commented that although his bodily remains are at Wildji, his power is in his clan Country at Mangulwan. It would be to Mangulwan that Bill would have to go if he wanted to have Namadbara 'come out' and communicate with him.

Namadbara's post-death influence

The several Western Arnhem Landers who were particularly close to Namadbara felt that the specialness of his powers was so great that he ought to go on and live, perhaps forever. For Big Bill, it would seem that Namadbara represented a peak of Aboriginal achievement:

'Uncle?' I said. 'You bin know everything. Why don't you stay forever? You ought to stay, because, Uncle, you got everything.'

'My boy,' he said, 'If I oughta break that law, but I can't do it. We all going. World too strong, earth too strong. I couldn't, I gotta go. The law — every one of us. Old people went — I gotta go. The world and Bininj [people]. We gotta get old, we gotta go. No matter who people — good [whether they're good], another man good, good, good, that same way we [all] go.'

He said, '[But] I'll be around somewhere. I'll be waiting, but you can't see me. I'll be watching you.'

A similar understanding about Namadbara's continuing to exist is voiced by Ron Cooper:

He's in Arnhem Land somewhere. I feel that he's somewhere, that he's there. I haven't met him, but he's there somewhere.

IAN: *So that Old Man said that he wouldn't . . . like, did you say that he wouldn't die? Or, that he would die, but he would . . . ?*

But he would live in somebody else. He would come back into somebody else.

In the same vein, expressing a concept of reincarnation, Big Bill said that Namadbara told him that we change bodies 'like changing a shirt'.

Bill records his memory of a conversation he and Namadbara had had in the days not long before he died. At the time, they were at a camp on the beach, near Coombe Point:

He told me, 'I'm weak. I'm weak one now. You come hold my arm.' I used to holdem this arm, for blood [pulse]. 'He work? Feel it if he work.' 'Yeah, he work.' 'But not much, weak one.' He used to tellem me, 'Weak one. [In] two week, three week, I get sick.'

[Bill replies] 'But look [at] your body, you all right.' One week I went [at] three o'clock morning, four o'clock, wake. I went there.

'Uncle? You all right?'

Namadbara: 'Yeah. I'm all right.'

Bill: 'What happening now?'

Namadbara: 'No, one week more.'

Bill: I bin sorry.

Namadbara: 'Don't cry,' he said, 'Forget.'

Bill: But people bin sorry, sorry, sorry. And I think about sorry.

Finish then [he passed away].

[But Namadbara] he said, 'Don't do it. Forget. I'll be around somewhere.'

It was at Mangulwan in the mid-1980s that, some years after his death, Namadbara appeared to a buffalo shooter, a Balanda, one night at his campfire. Most of those who talked of Namadbara's life knew of this incident, and several gave accounts of it. This man was contracted to the Northern Land Council on the government-funded scheme (BTEC) to reduce the wild buffalo population, believed to be major carriers of the cattle diseases, brucellosis and tuberculosis. He was sitting at his fire boiling the billy when Namadbara walked into the circle of light, wearing a hat and carrying a walking stick. The following is a compilation from the separate accounts of two brothers, Johnny Williams and Nelson Mulurinj:

'What are you doing here?' he asked [of the Balanda], speaking English. 'I'm the boss of this land.'

The buffalo shooter answered, 'I'm working for Ada and Elsie, shooting buffalo.'

Director of the Australian Institute of Aboriginal Studies (now AIATSIS), Professor Neil W. G. Macintosh (middle), under the guidance and strict instructions from Namadbara (right), is conducted to the major sacred site complex of Awunbarna (Mt Borradaile) in 1971; he is also accompanied by lay missionary, Graham White (left). Photo: *Northern Territory Affairs*, vol. 7; published by Department of the Northern Territory, 1973–1975.

'That's my cousin and that's my daughter,' Namadbara told him.

That two bin sit down, have a cup of tea.

After that Namadbara said, 'I'm going now.' He walked four or five steps and then disappeared.

Not long after, Johnny Williams arrived at the contractor's camp to get fuel. The Balanda told him, 'Hey, I've just been talking to Old Man Compass.'

John told him, 'He died ten years ago.'

At this, the buffalo shooter got the wind up, packed up, and drove away.[62]

When I spoke to this man in January 1997, he was living in New Zealand. I had earlier written to him to let him know I had heard the story from local people and whether he himself had any knowledge of the particular incident. His response to my phone call stunned me. I had assumed, despite all the stories I had recorded, that he would have no knowledge of such an event. Instead, he said he *did* remember the incident and that it was an event in his life that was very special to him; he implied that he wished I hadn't heard the story. He added that he 'did not want it blown out of proportion — people wouldn't believe it'. He then ended the conversation rather abruptly, saying, 'I'm sorry, I don't want to say anything more about it.'

Namadbara's Legacy

All those who knew Namadbara during his life and who expressed an opinion about him as a marrkidjbu and as a fellow member of their community agreed that, as a powerful marrkidjbu, he was pre-eminent. 'Properly number one' was an often-used expression, as well as 'champion'. As Bluey Ilkgirr said:

Some people I know, they're clever orright. But he bin clever proper!

Several chose to make their assessment of his work and character by comparing him with Western religious figures or by using Christian terminology:

Nelson Mulurinj: Do you know Jesus? Well, he was like him.[63]

Ron Cooper: He was a prophet. A very holy man. He knew what was going to happen to the people. He had already seen that. To me, he was a saint. There's not a word like it. You know — say, we read in the Bible, we read about Jesus, we read about . . . But this man was a saint!

Jamesie Wauchope: He was a very wise, very powerful Old Man.

Bluey asked whether I knew the Bible story of 'feeding the five thousand'. Bluey held out his finger to illustrate to me a tiny piece of bread:

Yet in the Bible, [Christ] could feed many, many people. Well, [Namadbara] same like that.

In the memories of Western Arnhem Landers recorded here, his reputation clearly was one of having achieved the highest status as a person of knowledge and influence.[64] He was treated with a respectful honour and deference that was unusual even among men of the highest ranking.

Tom Haydon, a non-Aboriginal film-maker who had dealings with Namadbara in the early 1970s, was very much struck by the deference paid to Namadbara.[65] His first meeting with him was on the beach at Wildji in Mountnorris Bay. He had arranged the meeting to negotiate with Namadbara about access to the Country around Mt Borradaile for the filming of *Long, Long Walkabout* (1974). Haydon waited there for Namadbara to arrive from nearby Croker Island and describes Namadbara getting out of the boat and walking the 50 or so metres across the sand to the shade where they were to have their discussions. Namadbara's presence was 'quite regal' Haydon said, as he made his way up the beach. He was wearing thongs out of which his feet kept slipping, and a young man crouching down beside him ran along and continually picked them up and placed them in front of him so that his feet would step back into them again, as he continued his slow walk up the beach. Haydon said he had parleyed with prominent senior Aboriginal men before, including a particular pre-eminent central Arnhem Land painter, but had 'never seen deferential behaviour to equal this before'. He said there was 'a very dramatic quality' to their negotiations on the beach, with Namadbara being 'immensely in command' and 'very with it' in terms of 'the questions and answers we had to go through'.

Namadbara, then, was roundly accorded the highest of status. Initially a healer, his activities encompassed much more and his reputation grew accordingly. His reputation was based on his ability to bring security into people's lives, especially during times of turbulent change, by providing the assurance of confident answers to otherwise uncertain outcomes and engaging people in actions that, if undertaken correctly, would ensure a positive outcome. His reputation was also based on demonstrations of his knowledge of the future — his ability to 'see' what lay ahead for the community; his successful healing of the sick; his decisive leadership; his ability to counter supernatural perils and evil magic (sorcery); and generally, through his wisdom in providing guidance to people, particularly in their unavoidable engagement with an outside and dominating culture. Thus, it could be said of Namadbara that he was indeed, to use Elkin's (1977) term, 'a man of high degree'.

People who gave accounts of Namadbara's life observed that there are no people today with such wide and commanding reputations as powerful practitioners. There are several who practice as marrkidjbu and have demonstrated a clear ability to heal, but it would seem there is now no viable niche in Western Arnhem society for the development of the marrkidjbu into the 'old-style, high-powered' practitioner who had such a significant role to play across most aspects of people's lives. The present-day practitioner does not have that same route to respected power and community influence that was once the case. The ideology underpinning this aspect of Western Arnhem life has been subverted or swamped by a

Western ideology — a materialist and more technologically complex culture that cannot conceive of, or does not 'believe' in, the existence or efficacy of the marrkidjbu's power. There are new and competing avenues for influence.

One elderly Gunbalanya woman, asked for her opinion about present-day marrkidjbu, declared disparagingly, 'Witchdoctors! Now we have the Church. Now we need have no fear . . . And we have the Health Clinic.' Nonetheless, based on Central Australian developments, there is potential for future cooperation between West Arnhem marrkidjbu and Western health agencies with consequent greater status for practising marrkidjbu (see NPY 2013; McCoy 2008).

Though no one of Namadbara's stature and power is alive today, his legacy lives on in the leaders he moulded and empowered, and in the respect and pride in Bininj culture, Bininj knowledge and Bininj ways that he engendered — not only among Aboriginal people, but among everyone who had interactions with him. In Jacob Nayinggul's words:

He set the foundations for the future — black and white going hand in hand together.

Gunbalanya/Oenpelli community from Injalak hill. Looking north across the floodplains towards Namadbara's Country beyond the far horizon.
Photo: Jason Motbey, 2008.

Afterword

My primary motivation in bringing the story of Paddy Compass Namadbara's life as a marrkidjbu to a wider public is to contribute to the growing respect that this facet of Aboriginal traditional life finally appears to be achieving (e.g. NPY 2013; San Roque 2011). This story demonstrates that as a clever man, Paddy Compass Namadbara possessed remarkable capacities to perceive events that others cannot, and to engage in extraordinary feats of healing and knowledge beyond the abilities of ordinary human beings. But these events raise challenging questions. If we in the West, as inhabitants of 'the Western mind' (Tarnas 1991), are to take these stories as seriously as the Western Arnhem Landers take them, and not dismiss or ignore them on account of their non-scientific status, then how are we to treat them? Generally, this 'knowledge' might be regarded as knowledge of a wider and more flexible reality and broader dimensions of existence than we in the Western world normally allow. Some have labelled this sort of knowing (as demonstrated by Namadbara) 'extraordinary knowing' (see Mayer 2008). As science continues to debate and develop new models of reality, our future understanding may yet accommodate these presently inexplicable phenomena.[66]

Whichever way one views them, stories such as Namadbara's clearly demonstrate a remarkable achievement of the human spirit. The psychotherapist Craig San Roque expressed this eloquently in a speech delivered at the 2011 World Council of Psychotherapy Congress in Sydney, in honour of the Sigmund Freud Award-winning Central Australian Ngaanyatjarra Pitjantjatjara Yankunytjatjara (NPY) ngangkari (traditional healer) team:

The award to the NPY ngangkari team is an acknowledgement of the existence and living practices of the ngangkari work throughout the Australian continent

. . . For how many generations — over how many millennia have these people held this line? Perhaps for 2000 generations. Time enough to establish an experiential evidence base, time enough to make mistakes and recover, time enough to learn how to help and heal bodymind, maintain cohesion of self/soul/family/Country through all the ups and downs of civilisation conserving itself within the unique conditions of this continent . . . Ngangkari have been working to heal and hold the integrity of kin and kurunpa[67] since before Mohammed, before Jesus and Mary, before Gautama Buddha . . . before perhaps the 10,000- or more year-old maternal nurturant cultures of the Black Sea and Old Europe . . . Before then maybe, ngangkari hold to a thread parallel perhaps to the shamanic lines of Northern Europe and Russia, mountain Tibet, Taoist China, Japan, the Americas, Pacific Polynesia and older . . . holding the genetic line which we all share . . . Surely this is something worth recognising? (San Roque 2011).

A.P. Elkin, in the reprint of his *Aboriginal Men of High Degree* (1977: 66), also wanted to express the extraordinary achievements of clever men such as Namadbara:

My object has been to show, firstly, that Aboriginal medicine-men, so far from being rogues, charlatans or ignoramuses, are men of high degree; that is, men who have taken a degree in the secret life beyond that taken by most adult males — a step which implies discipline, mental training, courage and perseverance. Secondly, that they are men of respect, and often of outstanding personality; thirdly, that they are of immense social significance . . . fourthly, that the various psychic powers attributed to them must not be too readily dismissed as mere primitive magic and 'make-believe,' for many of them have specialised in the workings of the human mind, and in the influence of mind on body, and mind on mind . . .

When I first encountered the stories of Paddy Compass in the late 1980s and early 1990s, I was struck by the enthusiasm of the storytellers and by the integrity with which they treated the special incidents they recalled about Old Man Compass. Around the same time, I read the observations from the Berndts (Berndt & Berndt 1970:145), as well as local Aboriginal leader Lazarus Lamilami (1974:134), about the diminishing number of high-powered marrkidjbu. By then, Namadbara had been dead for more than 10 years and there was only one roundly acknowledged powerful healer still operating in the region. The remaining clever ones, who were considered 'just ordinary', no longer had the same social niche necessary to become high-powered marrkidjbu, such as Namadbara. Taking my cue from Catherine Berndt's call for more research on Western Arnhem traditional 'doctors' and 'the powers they are believed to have' before such information disappears (Berndt 1984: 135), I took two years' leave from the Land Council and in

1995, enrolled as a Master of Arts candidate in anthropology at the University of Western Australia.

Over the following 18 months, I spent time in the main Western Arnhem communities — at Gunbalanya, Croker and Goulburn Islands, Cobourg Peninsula, Maningrida, and several of the community outstations, as well as Jabiru and Darwin — seeking out, recording and transcribing the stories about 'cleverness' and clever people, particularly Namadbara, and compiled this portrait of Paddy Compass.

During my work with the Land Council, 'the old people' came to know me well and were quite comfortable talking about esoteric matters. The events in these stories raised profound questions for me. Diagnosing illness by 'x-ray vision', bringing willy-willies into existence, bringing a dead animal back to life, knowing that someone a vast distance away has died long before the news arrives — how was I to make sense of this as a non-Aboriginal Westerner raised and educated within a standard Enlightenment tradition of reason, rationality and the separation of mind and matter? How might this be understood in terms of Western conceptions of reality? As eminent Sydney University anthropology Professor A. P. Elkin had wondered (Elkin 1977; Becket 1977; Wise 1985) and as the Berndts (Berndt & Berndt 1992:305) clearly contemplated, 'Is there something in it?' Is there a universal human capacity behind these phenomena?

In past ethnographic literature that touched upon the subject of clever men, they were frequently 'dismissed as frauds and humbugs', as Beckett (1977: x) noted, or as clever conjurers, and their claims of extraordinary activities and experiences quietly explained away — perhaps by the suggestion that they were psychologically unstable individuals (e.g. Cawte 1974:29). Generally, little attempt was made to take these claims seriously or deal with them in a non-dismissive way. In addition, where the matter has been dealt with in more detail, the material is presented as a generalised description, the ethnographer more interested, it would seem, in constructing generalisations about these activities ('Group X makes clever men this way; group Y does it in such and such a way'). Yet little sense of the individual practitioner is gained, nor are the particular experiences that went to make up that generalisation revealed.[68] Instead, one gains the impression from such accounts that there is a standardised and formal process in the making of a 'clever' person, an almost rigid format that is followed to achieve the particular results. My sense, however, is that the clever person is much more individualistic and experimental, resistant to a too-hurried generalization, responding instead in an innovative way to their individual experiences of their special ('otherworldly') realm, as well as to the historical moment, to the social circumstances of their day. The life of Paddy Compass as presented here through the eyes of his fellow Western Arnhem Landers is, I suggest, an illustration of this.

Max Charlesworth (1984), in calling for a more considered approach and change of attitude from scholars to 'primal religions' and to their practitioners, is emphatic that they are not 'baby religions' in comparison with major 'world' religions. They are not inferior or 'simple-minded'. Quoting Deakin, he points out that their practitioners and adherents 'are mature human beings with their own insights into life, their own profound thinkers, seers, mystics, saints . . . and their own contribution to make to the spiritual experience of mankind' (quoted in Charlesworth 1984:14). Certainly, the picture that Western Arnhem Landers draw of Namadbara suggests a man of vision and of powerful insights, not the psychological misfit to which some scholars would have the clever person reduced.

This project has been inspired by Elkin's pioneering work on Aboriginal clever men — *Aboriginal Men of High Degree,* first published in 1945 — and by his unshaken belief in the reality of their 'psychic' abilities, and his efforts (though unsuccessful at the time) in finding an explanation for them that was understandable in Western terms. The question that haunted and drove him, generated by his experiences with Aboriginal clever people, was: 'What are the powers of the human mind?'[69] However, the intellectual and scientific climate of the times, driven by a prevailing mechanistic scientific worldview, was decidedly unsympathetic.

Today the wheel is turning sharply. New approaches have arisen that may help shine a light on these 'powers of the mind' and perhaps offer a certain plausibility. Science now regards the mind — or more generally, 'consciousness' — as a legitimate area of research (e.g. Blackmore 2012; Chalmers 1995; Snaprud 2018). 'Altered states of consciousness', a term unknown in Elkin's time and considered then as states evidencing a psychopathology (e.g. Cawte 1974; Wise 1985:241), have now been subject to a wide variety of research and discussion. As we have become more familiar with these altered states of consciousness, both theoretically and through our own subjective experiences, this has led to advancements in understanding the 'psychic' phenomena typically described within the arenas of healing, shamanism and clever practices in general (e.g. Tart 1972, 1980, 1998; Harner 1982; Bourguignon 1973; Noll 1985; Howell 1989; Nelson & Howell 1993–4; Winkelman 2010). Even so, it remains a contested area within academic considerations. Back in 1982, Marlene Dobkin de Rios (1982:45) pointed out that 'anthropological topics like witchcraft, sorcery, divination, and curing . . . have been studied anthropologically with old paradigms'. She considered that the 'totally new paradigm' in physics had important implications for anthropology and psychic phenomena in particular, arguing that 'it is only by attending to the shift in the nature of "reality" that we can benefit from our anthropological data bank to make sense out of [psychic] phenomena'.[70]

In researching these questions, I drew on the work of various anthropologists and social scientists, as well as debates among philosophers of consciousness, cognitive scientists and physicists, particularly regarding the nature of consciousness and of reality itself. In an attempt to understand the clever phenomena Paddy Compass exhibited, I examined literature discussing altered states of consciousness and associated research into so-called entheogens (psychoactive substances), current research within parapsychology, and the experiential findings from Eastern philosophies and practices regarding consciousness that have been emerging recently into Western discussions. I also examined some of the findings in the physical sciences and the various competing 'interpretations' of quantum mechanics and the question of the relationship between matter and consciousness that arises (see e.g. Barad 2007; Stapp 2007; Becker 2018).

Yet attempting to understand clever phenomena and entertaining such questions (rather than simply 'bracketing' them) remained a controversial approach. Anthropologist James Lett (1991:305), voicing a popular academic position, argued that the metaphysics contemplated by such considerations was fundamentally irrational. Nevertheless, he posed the pertinent question:

Are [what he called] paranormal phenomena real? The question is far from insignificant for anthropology. If human beings do have [these] capacities then our anthropological understanding of human nature is seriously deficient. The paranormal [presents a] challenge to the validity of our knowledge about human nature.

Even so, Lett (1991:319) maintained that scientific investigation had already demonstrated 'magical ideas [to be] incontestably false'.

This ambivalence is compounded by the fact that, from time to time, Australian anthropologists, archaeologists, linguists, and other fieldworkers themselves experience extraordinary and inexplicable events or observe such events while working in the field with Aboriginal people. Archaeologist Scott Cane's extraordinary encounter with a Tjukurrpa — a spiritual manifestation — while documenting Native Title claims with Pila Nguru men in Western Australia's Great Victoria Desert is one example. As Cane explains, at one point he and the party of Pila Nguru men arrive at the shore of the first of two salt lakes — both are sacred, he tells us, and a source of ceremonially valued clay oxides (Cane 2002: 28–29):

The men covered themselves with ochre in preparation for ceremonial activity. I watched them from the back seat of my vehicle where I sat with an elderly man named Bobby Jones. Bobby has since died and was then in a very fragile state. I looked at his face. His eyes were bare, looking beyond my stare, glassy and a little frightening. Once the ritual decoration was complete the men moved in ceremonial order across the lake and through the vegetated peninsula towards the second lake. I left the car and walked with them. We walked in song through the mallee covering the peninsula until the escarpment came into view. To my surprise a man lay wailing at [its] base. It was Bobby Jones. His cry pierced us across the open distance. Proceeding towards Bobby all the men began to wail. Bobby's eyes and cheeks were wet with tears, his eyes black and distant. What had happened between the time I left Bobby's side in the car and joined the ceremonial procession? Could this elderly man have snuck away, unnoticed by me, and raced with Olympic speed across the two lakes to the escarpment?

Cane is completely nonplussed by this event. In an attempt to understand it, he refers to A. P. Elkin's *Aboriginal Men of High Degree* and his description of 'fast travelling': 'I had always thought such stories to be complete nonsense. Now I was not so sure. I am not sure what took place at the salt lakes.'

A second event occurs towards the end of their mapping trip (Cane 2002:30–32):

Our food was out and water was low. Other than stale damper crusts, I had not eaten for days. On the last day we visited a cave in the hills where we [he and the only other non-Aboriginal in the party] were forced to run at speed into its dark uneven recesses, and where each of us was grabbed unexpectedly and rammed violently, as if in a rugby tackle, face down onto the dusty floor . . . That night we camped near a low hill . . . a location at which three Tjukurrpa — spiritual manifestations — intersect and said to be a very [spiritually] dangerous place . . . It was a freezing desert night . . . Stirring sometime after midnight, cold in my swag, I stoked the fire and looked around. Simon Hogan, who was born at this place, was sitting up at Ian's campfire looking at me. I gazed back from the warmth of my swag . . . He was sitting naked next to the fire . . . Ian Baird [the other non-Aboriginal] was asleep on the other side of the fire . . . Hours later I stirred again . . . Simon was still sitting naked straight backed, at his fire . . . Shortly before dawn I got up and urinated . . . Simon was still awake and I watched him across my shoulder . . . I fell back to sleep and then overslept. [Waking] I walked over to Ian's camp [and remarked on Simon's presence all night at Ian's campfire]. Ian looked surprised. No one, he said, was camping or sitting next to him . . . In fact he had seen Simon Hogan sleeping three camps away. I thought Ian was teasing and pressed the point.

Scott and Ian went over to Simon's camp and Simon insisted he slept right where he was. Several days later, perplexed and pursuing the matter with the men back at their community, they explain to Cane:

'That's the Tjukurrpa,' and laughed as if to say 'funny coincidence', because the Tjukurrpa I saw 'does look a lot like Simon.' . . . Someone asked if I had seen the other two. No, I said surprised, and was told they were sitting just two camps to the west of me. Some of the men wondered why I hadn't seen the others and looked at me pityingly. Their eyes expressed surprise and disappointment as it dawned on them that I really didn't have a clue what the Tjukurrpa was. Had I been in the bush all this time and didn't know? I had thought I knew . . . but, until then, I had never entertained the potential of its actual spirituality.

Confronted by their own Western scientific-based understanding of reality, researchers who experience such incidents find it easier to dismiss them as 'impossible.' Consequently, they are either not reported at all or reported without any elaboration. They are not taken as a signal to question our own common understanding of reality. There is also an unspoken rule that to be taken seriously, it is best not to raise the question of the 'reality' of such phenomena. However, given the variety and breadth of these recorded experiences, in my view the question is quite reasonable and one that might be posed without prejudicial attack or derision (see Nadasdy 2007:36). A further problem is the fierce division in public and scientific debate between staunch sceptics and debunkers and those blithely indulging in unbridled speculations. It is feared that supporting any serious discussion of these scientifically 'anomalous' phenomena will legitimise purely religious beliefs. Therefore, anyone seeking insight into these phenomena must tread a fine line between these polarised positions.

I intended Namadbara's life-story to be part of a larger thesis aiming to explore if a wider framework for understanding these extraordinary events might provide insights and a possible ontological basis for their existence. Australian scholars, generally, had not attempted to situate Australian clever practices within a worldwide and cross-cultural frame of reference — for instance, within a context of shamanism 'writ large'[71] (Samuel 1993; see also Atkinson 1992; Sumegi 2013) — a frame that might finally allow theoretical development and a basis for understanding such practices in Western terms. Instead, the practices and experiences recorded by anthropologists and fieldworkers over the years have been treated in isolation. This is partly that Australian scholarship has focused, not on the ontological question of this clever power, but rather simply on the institution of the healer/sorcerer in Aboriginal society, and how this institution and role functions in Australian Aboriginal society. Elkin of course is the exception (along with international scholar, Eliade 1964, 1968). Elkin (1977:64) sought understanding from Tibetan Buddhist practices, via such information as existed in the 1930s and 1940s: 'We may derive from them some understanding of the Australian phenomena'. However, until recently, no one had followed this lead. Now, there is a plethora of relevant information emerging from scientific interaction with traditional Buddhist experiential-based philosophy (see e.g. Varela 1997; Thompson 2015; Wallace 2000). There was clearly room for focused research with the potential for deeper insights through wider contextualisation. Indeed, in pursuing that wider cross-cultural approach I found compelling resonances with Paddy Compass's story among the great stories of shamans, medicine-men and healers around the world and across a wide variety of quite different cultures (e.g. Katz 1982, 1989; Shirokogoroff 1999; Siskin 1983; Hultkrantz 1988; Murphy 1964; Hoppal & Howard 1993). These similarities raise many questions, among them the possibility that they represent common encounters with another aspect or dimension of reality yet to be understood (Nadasdy 2007; Hume 2007; Harner 1982). McClenon (1993: 109), for instance, argues: 'If these [common experiences and events] were totally a product of socialisation we would expect each group to produce distinct forms of anomalous events, since each culture has unique features. It is therefore reasonable to argue that belief proceeds, to a degree, from experience rather than being fully a product of socialisation' (see also Nadasdy 2007: 26). Atkinson (1992), in her study of shamans and shamanism, conjectured that these commonalities across cultures might indicate a human 'universal psychobiological capacity'.

I found that clever abilities have been recorded all over the world, not only among indigenous communities, but also within the classical Asian traditions. Written records of these 'psychic' phenomena (produced, it is claimed, through rigorous and disciplined mental and physical practices) go back almost 2000 years to the yoga sutras of Patanjali (Chaudhuri 2002). These sutras reveal a number of phenomena that seem to parallel some of those observed and recorded by ethnographers of Aboriginal Australia over the past 100 years (such as telepathy, 'out-of-body' experiences, knowledge of distant happenings, 'clairvoyance' and 'precognition'). These abilities or 'powers' are known as *siddhis* in the Sanskrit of ancient India. Although long ignored in the West, they are now receiving increasing scholarly attention (e.g. Jacobsen 2012; Kripal 2012; Kelly & Whicher 2015). Speaking of the mind-training of Tibetan monks and the subsequent development of *siddhis*, the scholar and Tibetan Buddhist practitioner, B. Alan Wallace (1999:185), reports: 'Once one has accomplished *samatha* [a complete and stable meditative quieting of the mind] various forms of extrasensory perception and paranormal abilities can be developed with relative ease . . . For an intelligent person educated in the modern West, one's first reaction to such claims may be to dismiss them without a second thought.' However, as Wallace points out, 'Many of the Buddhist contemplatives . . . have engaged in rigorous, sustained, attentional training that are either undeveloped or long forgotten in the West. In short, they have run experiments in consciousness that are unknown to modern science.'

Seeking further understanding, I was drawn into a deeper consideration of 'reality' and consciousness and whether there was a way of viewing reality that might legitimately support an understanding of these clever phenomena. In the physical sciences, quantum physicists now question and debate the role that consciousness may play in their measurements of quantum states. Some believe consciousness and matter to be inextricably entangled (Stapp 2007a, 2007b; Linde 1998; Rosenblum & Kuttner 2011; see also Kaiser 2012; Musser 2015). There is now no consensus about these two fundamental aspects of existence — the nature of consciousness, the nature of reality (Tarnas 1991; Fuchs 2015; Frank 2017).[72] Given this lack of consensus, the question of 'the powers of the mind' remains open and worthy of continued investigation (see Rosenblum & Kuttner 2011:255). My study suggests they deserve more attention and that to ignore existing insights into consciousness from non-Western sources may be denying ourselves further understanding of the nature of human beings and human cultures.

Summing up an anthropological forum on the 'supernatural', Susan Sered (2003:213) asked: 'Can we ever understand phenomena that we ourselves have never experienced?' Some anthropologists have deliberately opened themselves to these experiences, guided by their indigenous instructors. In doing so, they have encountered 'anomalous' experiences themselves (Laderman 1993; Turner 1993; Glass-Coffin 2010:207; Rocha 2017; Katz 1989; McCaul 2008; Winkelman 2010; Kahn 2014; Young & Goulet 1994). Although such experiences can be dismissed as merely 'anecdotal evidence', I suggest that an equally valid point is the one made, for example, by anthropologist Geoffrey Samuel (2013:249) in his considerations of Asian 'subtle-body' practices and concepts.[73] He writes:

> The willingness of significant contemporary thinkers to take [Asian 'subtle-body'] concepts seriously suggests that in ignoring the subtle body as a relic of obsolete modes of thought, or as a marginal fantasy of occult and New Age writers, we may be missing something of real value.

He makes the further point (2013:1):

> Whether or not we regard these concepts as referring in some way to real phenomena within human experience, the wide range of time and space within which they have been evidenced surely implies there is something there worth studying . . . It no longer makes sense simply to dismiss these practices as unscientific or nonsensical, but it is far from easy to know how to understand them.

Further experiential evidence is coming from entheogenic studies (involving researchers' experiences with psychoactive substances, e.g. recent research into plant-based entheogens ayahuasca and DMT) (e.g. Rodd 2011; St John 2015) as well as from other research including 'psychedelics' (Pollan 2018; see also Hume 2007), disciplined personal practising of Tibetan Buddhist and other Eastern meditation techniques (Laughlin 1994) and modern Western magic-witchcraft-pagan techniques (Greenwood 2000; 2006; Hume 1997), to name a few. This contributes to our ideas, understanding and experience of what consciousness is, or can be, and adds to our appreciation of indigenous exploration, discoveries and knowledge in this area. Given the findings and prospective new models of understanding of consciousness that arise from this research, we are now in a position, as Hume (2002) has suggested, to reassess Aboriginal psychic data, data that has long lain dormant in ethnological texts.

It is often said that claims of extraordinary phenomena — things that are hard to believe — require extraordinary scientific evidence. However, it may also be kept in mind the possibility that certain of our human senses have been forgotten, perhaps atrophied, in our contemporary living, thus having the consequent effect of actually making things 'hard to believe'. In this respect, a very interesting reflection comes from the Canadian author, Sharon Butala (2005:139–148):

> I believe that areas of the body other than the recognised five senses are able to apprehend information about the world which often is not available through the acknowledged senses . . . I begin to think that our technological prowess has outstripped, overwhelmed and in some cases destroyed abilities which we all once had, and which people who remain close to Nature have maintained . . . Why should not we [technological moderns] be more capable of being tuned in to [nature] . . . ? If, put in a natural environment, being still and alert to new sensation, expecting only whatever happens and nothing more nor less, accepting such sensation as real and acting on it gives us new information about the world and/or extends our understanding of our place in creation, then it seems to me a practice worth pursuing. It may be that most people are so tense, so bombarded by other external stimuli and so disbelieving, such hard-core materialists, that they simply don't notice intuition when it does strike. It is possible if we spent more time alone and in Nature our intuitive abilities — another way of gathering information about the world — would strengthen . . . I practised inner stillness in order to hear, really hear, the wind, birdsong, whatever else might be in the air . . . I had a sense of my 'awareness' going out of me and not of these things entering me, but of me going out to mingle with them . . . Then I thought, this must be how Aboriginal hunters did it, by mingling with Nature in this way and thus knowing where the animals are and what they are doing . . . I have begun to think of this as 'throwing' one's consciousness . . . You have to be still and quiet for these things to happen; you have to release your expectations; you have to stop thinking you already know things, or how to categorize them, or that the world has already been explained and you know those explanations. You know nothing. You understand nothing. You have only what your own body tells you . . . Teach me is what you should say, and, I am listening . . . In a word: humility. Then things come to you as they did not when you thought you knew.

In his foreword to psychoanalyst Elizabeth Mayer's book, *Extraordinary Knowing*, a compelling investigation of psychic phenomena and extrasensory perception (ESP), eminent American physicist Freeman Dyson sums up his own stance on the matter (Mayer 2008:ix–xi):

> As a scientist I don't believe the story . . . on the other hand, as a human being I find the story convincing . . . There are three possible positions that one may take concerning the evidence for ESP. First, the position of orthodox scientists, who believe that ESP does not exist. Second, the position of true believers, who believe that ESP is real and can be proved to exist by scientific methods. Third, my own position, that ESP is real, as the anecdotal evidence suggests, but cannot be tested with the clumsy tools of science. These positions imply different views concerning the proper scope of science. If one believes . . . that the scope of science is unlimited, then science can ultimately explain everything in the universe, and ESP must either be non-existent or scientifically explainable. If one believes, as I do, that ESP exists but is scientifically untestable, one must believe that the scope of science is limited. I put forward, as a working hypothesis, that ESP is real but belongs to a mental universe that is too fluid and evanescent to fit within the rigid protocols of controlled scientific testing. I do not claim that this hypothesis is true . . . [but] that it is consistent with the evidence and worthy of consideration.

Clearly, there are no strictly scientific 'explanations' of the clever phenomena in Paddy Compass Namadbara's story. However, there are now many avenues of scientific research and first-person experiential evidence that provide valuable insights and proffer the possibility of understanding how extraordinary phenomena may come about. In highlighting such research, perhaps the common attitude of a priori dismissal or hard scepticism may be softened and frameworks of understanding developed in line with these bourgeoning research findings. In this respect, I find Bruce Kapferer's conclusion to the introductory chapter of his edited volume *Beyond Rationalism* encouraging (Kapferer 2003:25):

> My aim here has been to outline an approach towards magic and sorcery that encourages a redrawing of their significance — not for an anthropology that mindlessly and resolutely holds on to a traditionalist exoticism, but rather for an anthropology that is committed to radically questioning conventional understanding of what it means to be a human being and to extend towards new horizons of knowledge.

In presenting Paddy Compass Namadbara's story to a wider public, I would hope to encourage a more generous and open-minded view towards these abilities and capacities. Traditional healers are still practising within Aboriginal Australia and Aboriginal people can only benefit from a wider acknowledgement of these abilities. Following the lead in Central Australia (NPY 2013; Rothwell 2003), they may also benefit from these practices being included in the services offered to Aboriginal people by Western health agencies.

Acknowledgements

A research grant from the Australian Institute of Aboriginal and Torres Strait Islander Studies (AIATSIS) supported the 1995 fieldwork component involved in the project. My thanks to Stephen Wild for his efficient administering of the grant and his prompt attention to problems as they arose in the field. My 1995–6 research was undertaken as an MA student in the Department of Anthropology, University of Western Australia, where I received much encouragement and staunch support from my supervisors, Victoria Burbank and Bob Tonkinson — which is deeply appreciated. I also thank the UWA Department of Anthropology for its financial contribution to my fieldwork research. And my thanks to Nicolas Peterson and Isabel McBryde who provided referee support for my Australian Postgraduate Award scholarship application, an Award which allowed me to take two years' leave from the Land Council and commence my thesis research — an investigation of traditional healers and healing practices in Western Arnhem Land.

Focussing on the wider thesis issues meant that I put the story of Paddy Compass itself aside until I could complete the necessary background research. I did not have the opportunity to pick it up again until 2011 on my retirement and, particularly, after having been stimulated by anthropologist Susan Greenwood's *The Anthropology of Magic* (2009) and the correspondence and mutual support that followed. I thank Susan Greenwood for the inspiration.

Seven people participated in providing substantial accounts of their observations of Namadbara's feats of 'cleverness' and their memories of particular incidents and I thank them very much for trusting me with their stories. Others provided shorter comments and viewpoints. My thanks to them all for entrusting me with their stories.

Acknowledgements

I am very much in debt to the late George Chaloupka for his kind provision of his 1973 photographs of Namadbara, and also to Namadbara's sister, the late Ada Brown, and his grandson, the late Tim Mamikba, for their permission to use them.

Thanks is also due to:

Murray Garde, particularly for his linguistic expertise; also Peter Cooke, Ian McIntosh, Jacob De Hoog, Alan Randall, Lynne Hume, Sandy Toussaint, Kim McCaul, Amy Roberts, Allan Marett, Nic Peterson, Geoffrey Samuel, Nancy Williams, the late Joel Kahn, Susan Greenwood, Michael Harner, Paul Nadasdy, Ross Bolleter, Julie Gittus, Scott Cane, Frances Wade, Jan Wositsky, Bruce Birch, Sabine Hoeng, Annie Sjostrom, Daryl Wesley, Eva Purvis, Don Christophersen, Carlo Canteri, Allie Dawe, Rosie Elliott and Gwyneth Trysant for moral support and for reading the manuscript and for critical and encouraging comments. I thank Simon Watkinson for his work on the maps. I would particularly like to thank my one-time NLC colleague, Ken Lum, for his constant and unstinting support, advice (sometimes unheeded) and encouragement through the early years of this project. Many thanks to Jane Cafarella for assistance in editing the afterword. Thanks also to Jo-Ann Christophersen and the staff at the NLC Jabiru office for their assistance, and to Justin O'Brien and the Gundjeihmi Aboriginal Corporation for additional office assistance. To my daughter, Lorraine Kabbindi White, my deep appreciation for her efforts in establishing and confirming consents from authors' families to publish their stories. Thanks also to Gabrielle O'Laughlin of Kakadu National Park for locating and providing photographs of several of the authors.

Paddy Compass Namadbara: A Putative Timeline

Many of the accounts of Namadbara's life do not indicate when they took place, so have not been included in this timeline.

1890	**c.1898:** Born at Jerauri on Cooper Creek
1900	**1912–1916:** Enters ceremonial seclusion (Ubarr) at Malay Bay
1910	**1917–1921:** Further period of seclusion
1920	**1925:** First encounter with power, the 'sugarbag event' **1925:** Acquisition of spirit children **1920s – early 1940s:** Worked on Reuben Cooper's timber mills: Iwalk, Marralkiny, Maliyirrkul and Inybarlmun
1930	**1920s – early 1940s:** Worked on Reuben Cooper's timber mills: Iwalk, Marralkiny, Maliyirrkul and Inybarlmun
1940	**1920s – early 1940s:** Worked on Reuben Cooper's timber mills: Iwalk, Marralkiny, Maliyirrkul and Inybarlmun **c.1940s:** Second encounter with power, speaking with the yumbarrbarr
1950	**1952:** Participates in first Kunabibi ceremony, at Gunbalanya **1950s–1960s:** Painting period, Croker Island **c.1958:** Initial 'cat event', inaugurating drum-burial rituals **Late 1950s–1970:** Period of drum-burial rituals
1960	**1950s–1960s:** Painting period, Croker Island **Late 1950s–1970:** Period of drum-burial rituals **1968–1972:** Active in formation of the First Aboriginal Mining Company (FAMCO); discussions with Tom Haydon on filming access for *Long, Long Walkabout* 1974
1970	**Late 1950s–1970:** Period of drum-burial rituals **12 August 1978:** Passes away, at Waliwanyun, Mountnorris Bay **1978:** Buried at Wanjurrk, Mountnorris Bay

Glossary

Note: the abbreviation AE indicates Aboriginal English. Unless otherwise specified, Aboriginal words are in Kunwinjku.

antbed	AE, both the earthy material comprising termite mounds and the termite mound itself (so-called 'anthill')
Balanda	non-Aboriginal person; term usually reserved for a person of European descent
Bininj	a Kunwinjku (Bininj kunwok) term meaning a male person; also refers to Aboriginal people in general (i.e. male and female) as opposed to non-Aboriginal
bin	AE, a past tense marker
Board of Conservation	the Board of Management of the Gurig National Park, Cobourg Peninsula; under joint management arrangements between NT government (Conservation Commission of the Northern Territory) and traditional owners
Bunidj	clan name
business	AE, ceremony
cheeky	AE, something that is dangerous in its effect if eaten or imbibed without special preparation, or for someone in terms of their actions
clever	AE, term used to distinguish someone with the special ability to demonstrate 'magical' or 'psychic' phenomena; also a person with this power. See also *marrkidjbu* and *nakordangyi*.
countryman	AE, used fairly loosely to refer to someone, male or female, who may share the same language, same cultural practices, or the same clan-land as the speaker
daluk	a female adult
djang	'The spiritual essence' left behind by Creation Ancestors
djura	Macassan loan word: paper, pieces of paper; a term common to all the Western Arnhem Land language groups
donga	widespread north Australian term, used by non-Aboriginal and Aboriginal speaker alike, for a demountable dwelling, a small cabin, or substantial bush hut
duwa	one of two patrimoieties; see under *Nabulanj/Ngalbulanj*
heart-crack	AE, to receive a bad shock or experience sudden and extreme fright
Ildukidj	clan name
kubbulak	variety of *sugarbag*

Kamulkban	clan name
kill	AE, to hit and knock out or make unconscious (in comparison to 'killim dead' — to kill)
konjdja	antbed, red antbed. See also *antbed*.
kumula	a power, usually considered to be conferred by a clever person, gifted to a person to enhance an already existing capacity or skill
Kunabibi	the major *duwa* moiety regional annual ceremony; introduced into Western Arnhem Land in the 1950s
kunbalem	the fat of an animal or person
kunbang	alcohol
kundjak	a form of sacred and dangerous power
kundulk	a Kunwinjku general term for a tree, but also used for various wooden objects, e.g. a coffin
kunkidj	see *mankarni*
kunmalng	a person's 'soul', spirit, breath or vital-force
kunmokurrkurr	the patri-recruited social grouping that is commonly referred to in English as a clan-group
kunrurrk	a house or dwelling
kurrwilluk	curlew bird
Lorrkon	mortuary ceremony where the deceased's bones are placed in a hollow-log coffin
maam	Iwaidja, the Kunwinjku equivalent is *nakidjkidj*. See *namorrorddo*.
mah	'okay' as in 'okay let's do it', 'okay you can have it', etc.
mandjanek	see *marrwakani*
Manilakarr	clan name
mankarni	a variety of sorcery practice
mankordang	the clever, magic or psychic power possessed by a clever person; synonymous with *marrngkidj*
mankung	Kunwinjku term for bush honey, *sugarbag*, that is produced by several different species of native bee; each species produces a distinct variety of honey
Marrayin	a major regional ceremony associated with both *duwa* and *yirridjdja* moieties

marrkidjbu	a person, male or female (though there being far fewer female practitioners), who has the special power (*marrngkidj* or *mankordang*) that includes the ability to heal, or equally, to harm another — the term does not distinguish how the power is used in practice
marrngkidj	the 'clever', magic, or psychic power possessed by a clever person; the special power of a *marrkidjbu*; synonymous with *mankordang*
marrwakani (Iwaidja)	the 'cheeky' yam, *Typhonium* sp. (*mandjanek* in Kunwinjku)
Minjilang	Croker Island
Morak	a major regional ceremony associated with both *duwa* and *yirridjdja* moieties
Murran	clan name
Nabulanj/ Ngalbulanj; Nakangila/ Ngalkangila	The full western Kunwinjku patrilineal subsection system terms, organised within two patrimoieties, *yirridjdja* and *duwa*, as follows, where na- indicates male and ngal- female: Duwa moiety Yirridjdja moiety na/ngal – bulanj na/ngal – kangila na/ngal – kodjok na/ngal – wamud na/ngal – ngarridj na/ngal – wakadj na/ngal – bangardi na/ngal – kamarrang
nakidjkidj	Kunwinjku. See under *namorrorddo*. The Iwaidja equivalent is maam.
namarnde	often translated by AE speakers as 'devils', implying that they are something to be very wary of; however, can also refer loosely to a dead person's spirit, as well as to the helping 'spirit familiars' such as Namadbara's two 'children'
namorrorddo	Kunwinjku term referring to usually malicious, non-human beings, 'spirits', often called 'shooting star spirits'; described as having long claws and trails of white light streaming from their heads. They may steal a person's spirit (*kunmalng*) and, unless it is retrieved, the person will die; they come to feast on the human body the day after death and are said to be similar to the being called nakidjkidj [Kunwinjku; maam in Iwaidja] and so may share nakidjkidj association with the power of sorcerers and clever people. Yumbarrbarr is the Iwaidja equivalent
na-kordang-yi	equivalent to *marrkidjbu*, a person with the power (*mankordang*) to heal (or harm) another person. Literally 'male person-magical power-with'
ngalyod	The Rainbow Serpent — both the fundamental creative expression of continuing life and at the same time its original initiator, the bringer of life to Western Arnhem Land; the concept of *ngalyod* is also tied up with the clever person's ability to wield power — a power available to those clever enough to harness, control and possess it. *Ngalyod* can be sent out of the body for magical healing or harming purposes and can be drawn out of bodies of water where they usually reside to be used for the purposes of the clever person

ngangkari	Central Australian Ngaanyatjarra Pitjantjatjara Yankunytjatjara term for traditional healer
ngordmang	to heal by sucking on the skin and spitting out blood
njamed	Kunwinjku, meaning 'whatsaname', 'thingamajig'
OAM	Medal of the Order of Australia
olguman	AE, old woman
Old Man	an honorific in Western Arnhem AE, thus the capitalisation when used in direct speech, as in 'Hey, Old Man'
outstation	small Aboriginal homeland community
savvy	a loan word adopted into AE, to understand
silly	AE, has a stronger meaning than in Standard English, here it can carry the sense of something sinister
skin	a person's subsection identity; see above at *Nabulanj/Ngalbulanj*
sugarbag	AE, honey produced by native bees
Ubarr	(Iwaidja: *Kuwalk/Wuwalk*) a now-defunct major regional Western Arnhem ceremony prior to the introduction of Kunabibi
willy-willy	general Australian term for a little whirlwind; in the text it is a manifestation of the controlled power of the clever man
wurdwurd	Kunwinjku: children; in the text it refers to the 'spirit children' who were the spirit helpers of Namadbara
Wuwalk	see *Ubarr*
yirridjdja	one of two patrimoieties; see under *Nabulanj/Ngalbulanj*
Yulukidj	clan name
yumbarrbarr (Iwaidja)	see *namorrorddo*

Endnotes

1. That is, the patrilineal landowning group (Berndt & Berndt 1970:54ff), known in Iwaidja as namanamadj and in Kunwinjku as kunmokurrkurr. The land or 'estate' of Namadbara's Alarrdju clan is known by its 'big name' (Berndt & Berndt 1970:54) as Mangulwan and includes and encompasses the area known by Europeans as Mt Permain and by the Iwaidja as Lanka (Lamilami 1974:26). Note: in an Iwaidja orthography recently established by linguist Bruce Birch, this is rendered 'Ldanka'.
2. Wilambilam and Namadbara's mothers were sisters; the two men thus had the same subsection 'skin' (nabulanj), one's subsection being pre-determined by that of the mother.
3. That is, 'workers' in the European sense. Those on the northern coast had an established tradition of providing labour for visiting Macassans in return for desired goods. However, Macassan visits officially ceased in 1907 (Macknight 1976).
4. See e.g. Lamilami (1974: 155), and compare Levitus (1995: 69) who uses the term 'a fossicking economy' to describe this engagement.
5. Reuben Cooper was the son of Englishman Joel Cooper and a Cobourg Peninsula Iwaidja woman Alice Marawuldan. His father sent him to Adelaide to be educated and he later returned to take over the timber mill business and other enterprises begun by his father. It was a fairly regular group of typically Iwaidja people who provided the necessary labour. See Mulvaney and Calaby (1985:301–302); Hill (1951); Lamilami (1974:181); Whimpress and Cooper (2018).
6. Examples of his paintings along with those of other Croker Island painters can be viewed online. See e.g. https://www.aboriginal-bark-paintings.com/namatbara/ and also the National Museum of Australia 'Old Masters' exhibition website: www.nma.gov.au/exhibitions/old_masters/artists/paddy_compass_namatbara
7. This particular Kunabibi, the first to have been performed at Oenpelli, has been said to have been at the behest of anthropologist Ronald Berndt. See also Cole (1979:48).
8. In Western Arnhem Land, 'women had a minor healing role . . . the main [marrkidjbu] identified in myth and in everyday life were men' (Berndt 1984:127). This is in contrast to the situation apparent in Central Australia — see NPY (2013). For general discussion of similar concepts of 'power' world-wide; see e.g. Harvey (2006:129–134).
9. This account is generalised from the accounts of Bluey Ilkgirr, Thompson Yuludjiri and Robert Djorlom, responding to my questions, 'Did he ever say how he got that power, how he became clever?' Each agrees in the basic outline of what happened, and differ mainly in that one may add some details that another lacks.
10. The honey, mankung, from the native bee. In this case it was thought to be the kubbulak variety (Iwaidja korlerrardbe).
11. The concept of stingless native bees 'biting' is there in Iwaidja lore — in the story 'The First Bees', Gubalag (kubbulak) bit the other two bee men, Nabiwu (nabiwo) and Gadderi (kardderre) (see Berndt & Berndt 1992:393).
12. See also Petri (2014:10); Sumegi (2013:69) describes a Tibetan shamanic experience where an apparent similar state of consciousness is described as 'not regarded as ordinary sleep or a state of mere unconsciousness'.
13. It is not clear whether the following occurred immediately after he had been 'bitten' or during the period he was 'asleep' after he had returned to camp.
14. This appears to be a 'rule' of the spirit world, as explained to me, that a person cannot, or is unable to, communicate directly through speech with the spirit of a dead person — at least not in the initial meeting. They can only nod their head in response.
15. In Bluey Ilkgirr's account, these last two words were drawn out and emphasised to indicate the extra-ordinariness of the encounter.
16. These songs, which belong to Alarrdju clan, were revealed to Namadbara in spirit encounters such as this. One of his brothers was also a receiver and singer of these songs.
17. The concept of children spirit familiars is similar in Eastern Arnhem Land, where they are called djamarrkuli or manggata (Reid 1980:95, 1983:33, 37). Compare also with the rai spirit children concept of the Kimberley (Coate 1966–7:96) and Glaskin (2008:45).
18. In English, Western Arnhem Landers make the distinction by calling these namarnde 'devils.'
19. This is based on transcripts of two interviews with Bill, in 1988 and 1995.

20 It seems that these events took place later in Namadbara's life. It is said to have occurred when Namadbara was working at one of the timber mills run by Reuben Cooper, sometime in the early 1940s, as Reuben died in 1942. However, Hoeng (n.d.) presents argument that 1950 is a more likely estimate for Namadbara's acquisition of this 'higher level of power'.

21 Yumbarrbarr in Iwaidja and namorrorddo in Kunwinjku; often called a 'shooting star spirit', it is said to be similar to nakidjkidj. Berndt and Berndt (1970) describe nakidjkidj as the 'patron' of sorcerers. See also Berndt, Berndt and Stanton (1982:125) and Birch (2011: 318–319), and see Lamilami (1974:20–22) for a description of a yumbarrbarr.

22 There is an interesting ethnographic parallel in Harner (1982:xv). He reports that, among the Conibo of the Upper Amazon, in learning to become a shaman 'learning from trees' is considered superior to learning from another shaman. See Birch (2011:318) for yumbarrbarr connection with trees.

23 See also Tonkinson (1991:130) re 'power' as willy-willy.

24 The power to kill someone or something and then bring them back to life is also noted among Kimberley clever men's abilities (Coate 1966–7:98–99).

25 While kundulk means 'tree', the word is also used for various wooden objects, e.g. coffin.

26 See Lamilami (1974:132) for a version of this practice.

27 Interestingly, Eastwell (1982a:232) refers to information from 'a very old informant' [unfortunately without indicating from what region] about a word that Eastwell says denotes 'soul-loss illnesses'. He writes, 'The word refers to the filaments secreted by an insect which are joined by the native healer to form a long string which, when attached to the patient and a nearby tree, provides a track for the patient's departed spirit to return.'

28 Compare Chaloupka et al. (1985:101) 'string' = bunbun. See Taylor (1987:243, 307, 309), who was told that it is the clan's life essence that resides in each clan member's bones while they are still living. Further, if namorrorddo is able to steal this 'soul', this then subverts the normal cycle of the reincarnation of this clan soul back to the clan site (djang). In contrast, Taylor was informed that wayarra are the profane spirits of the dead humans. They look like skeletons and linger within the bones of the deceased.

29 Speaking of Yolngu practices, Reid writes: 'Whereas the sorcerer uses heat and fire to enhance the effectiveness of his techniques, the healer utilises the healing qualities of cool water in his work. If the healer extracts an object he will always throw it in a lagoon or stream to annul its harmful power' (Reid 1983:83). See also Tonkinson (1984:232).

30 In his Mayali to English dictionary, Evans gives the following attestation: 'ngordmang = suck blood. Gurdangyi gabingordmang gulbba gaburriwe = The clever man sucks people's blood, and spits it out' (1991:404). See also Phillip Robert's account of his personal experience of this treatment (Lockwood 1962:19–21).

31 In her paper 'The role of native doctors in Aboriginal Australia', Catherine Berndt (1964:271), in referring to Western Arnhem Land states: 'In this region, there is less emphasis on sucking, massaging, and removal of objects than elsewhere . . . ' However, she particularly focuses on the practice of the two brothers, Namadbara and Wilambilam, who were undoubtedly the pre-eminent practitioners at Oenpelli at this time. I believe that she may have incorrectly assumed that their techniques were in fact the general practice, rather than a manifestation of the advanced skills of these two brothers. She also fails to recognise, or allow for the possibility, that the marrkidjbu may actually project or transmit his own energy or 'power' into the patient and achieve healing this way [in the same way, as it is now more widely known in the West, traditional Chinese healers, for instance, are said to project their 'chi' (glossed as 'vital internal energy') into a patient]. Compare the role of the 'miwi' in the Yaraldi system of practice (Berndt, Berndt & Stanton 1993). See also Tonkinson (1982:233) where the mabarn is described as imparting healing strength from his own body into that of the patient. This physical energizing of the patient may have a powerful beneficial and therapeutic effect, beyond the simply psychosomatic. Although Berndt describes a healing procedure by Wilambilam and actually writes 'he gave her strength — some of his own "spirit" or "power",' she does not, in the end, give this conception the consideration it deserves. Thus, it cannot so confidently be said, as Berndt claims (1964:280), that marrkidjbu 'were not equipped to cope with serious injuries or illness'. Thompson Yuludjiri's story of the spearing-healing incident discussed earlier, for instance, runs counter to that claim.

32 The same ability of healers is found throughout Aboriginal Australia, e.g. NPY (2013:184). The Central Australian ngangkari Rupert Langkatjukur Peter: 'Ngangkari have the same ability [as Western X-ray techniques] to see within a person . . . ' Elkin

(1977:166) writes: 'and the penetrating power of the "inner or strong eye" enables the medicine-man to see directly the condition of a sick person's "insides", without an X-ray machine and electric power.' See also Coate's (1966–7:101) translation of Mowaljarli's text: 'When people are sick and in pain the diagnosticians look through their flesh and see right inside their insides. They see their liver, intestines, their belly and their very soul. They see their diseases shining . . . the areas are opaque with blood, these organs look different.' Interestingly, Talbot (2011:184–185) cites several examples of Westerners using such 'internal vision' to successfully diagnose diseased internal organs, diagnosis which is later verified by medical examination.

33 In local Aboriginal English, 'silly' has a stronger meaning than in Standard English. Here it can carry the sense of something sinister, evil.

34 See Lamilami (1974:130–131) for a version of this practice. It is called kunkidj or marrkidj; compare with galka practices in eastern Arnhem Land: see Reid (1983:37). The term mankarni appears to be widespread. In the Borroloola region (600–700 kilometres to the southeast), it is the term used for a clever person. In western Queensland, according to Roth (1984 [1903]:34) it is the term for the bone-pointing equipment. This mankarni form of sorcery killing is similar to the Central and Western Desert 'featherfeet' traditions (see Berndt & Berndt 1992:324; Tonkinson 1978:111).

35 Compare this concept with, for example, Zen meditation practice, of 'settling the heart-mind.'

36 A highly speculative but nevertheless interesting account of why this might be so is provided by the Russian physicist Michael Mensky's 'extended interpretation of Everett's "many worlds" concept' within quantum theory. He speculates that, from his interpretative 'extension' of this concept, that within the unconscious or 'non-conscious' state (compare the state in which the clever person is typically 'made') knowledge is available and accessible from 'any time moments in future or past' (Mensky 2011:140).

37 Compare Berndt (1979:24): 'Among Gunwinggu speakers . . . a new spirit passes ill-intentioned guardians of the spirit world who attempt to do him harm.'

38 In August 1995, I visited this site (and Namadbara's Country generally) with Bill Neidjie. Bill wished to provide the opportunity for Namadbara to manifest himself and give Bill 'more story'. However, the occasion did not turn out as hoped. A pig-shooting contractor had set up at Mangulwan and had caged his pig-dogs around the favoured camping area. As the dogs appeared to be set to bark all night, Bill chose a less disturbed camp site a long way away from Mangulwan itself, and — combined with Bill's miserable flu — the situation was not conducive (said Bill) for 'good dreams'.

39 In terms of altered states of consciousness theory, a noise, such as the buzzing of bees or similar, is often the herald or initiator of the onset of an altered state of consciousness. See Hume (2002).

40 See Reid (1980:98;104) regarding her East Arnhem research: 'a marrnggitj has to be able to demonstrate his healing power to be accepted'. And see also Stephen (1979:14) who found (among the PNG Mae Enga people) that there was no ready acceptance of claims to otherworldly knowledge 'on the contrary, people are wary and sceptical of such experiences'. Elkin (1977:8) stated, 'A medicine man must be able to maintain his prestige . . . by success in his specialisation . . . otherwise faith in him will wane . . . '

41 In his later life, as Namadbara grew frailer, he frequented Gunbalanya less often and spent more and more time in small camps on the northwest Arnhem coast and on Croker Island.

42 Ron is referring to the joint management arrangements between traditional owners and the NT government (the Conservation Commission of the Northern Territory) and the Board of Management of the Gurig National Park, Cobourg Peninsula, which makes decisions on land-use issues.

43 Berndt (1964: 277) adds that this incident was acclaimed by the people as an example of accurate forecasting. In fact, while the barge *had* left Darwin, the stores did not ultimately arrive as expected; through misadventure, they ended up being abandoned along the way.

44 Compare Cawte (1964:186) for a West Kimberley account of the use of 'the snake' in the making and empowering of a 'doctor'; also Petri (2014).

45 A sharp object such as a stingray barb, or a piece of steel or wire that has been specially sharpened, for use in projective sorcery. See also Evans (1991:325). The term appears to be common to both eastern and Western Arnhem Land. Reid (1983:42) (manggimanggi) describes its use among Yolngu in the region of Yirrkala.

46 Compare this report with Elkin (1977:20): 'In western South Australia the postulant [is swallowed by a 'mythical snake' which] later ejects him in the form of a baby . . . ' This baby is then 'restored to man size by being sung . . . ' Also, Elkin (1977:22), referring to the Kimberley, writes, 'an old doctor takes the postulant reduced to the size of a baby to

the sky . . . '
47 See e.g. Reid 1980, 1983; Tonkinson 1982:232; Tonkinson 1991; Elkin 1977; Coate 1966–7:100.
48 Compare this event with a report referring to 'southwestern tribes' of Western Australia by Daisy Bates (1985:233). She states that, when a clever person dies (she refers to them as 'sorcerers'), the noise of the magic leaving the body can be heard. If there are other clever men present, they can pick up the magic, becoming doubly powerful in doing so. The occasion also presents the opportunity, she says, for a son of the dying clever man to 'catch his father's magic' and so become clever himself.
49 'Growem up' — typically this phrase is used to distinguish the role of a social (as opposed to paternal) father who has taken responsibility for all the matters involved in raising a child into adulthood. In this case Bluey is using it in a more general sense of Namadbara having had the role of a 'tribal father-figure' who has been their advisor, healer, leader and mentor.
50 On its vulnerability, see Tonkinson 1982:233; Akerman 1979; Clarke 2008:12; Petri 2014:11–12.
51 For other accounts of 'flying' or 'leaving one's body', see e.g. the account of Burrumarra's abilities before he came to the Galiwin'ku mission (McIntosh 1994:vii); Alan Ramsay's interview with David Mowaljarlai (Lommel & Mowaljarlai 1994); NPY (2013); Tonkinson (1984:232).
52 The eminent anthropologist, A.P. Elkin, whose ground-breaking book on clever men, *Aboriginal Men of High Degree*, was published in 1945, considered that: 'To reach [the] higher degree of psychic power by which one can send power out to bring life and death, to gain knowledge and to transfer thought without hindrance of time and space, and to see visions, requires much practice, courage and perseverance. Dangers and terrors must be faced — dangers of a psychic nature, the creation probably of one's own psychic exercise or of one's perception' (1977:58).
53 Namadbara is telling Bill that to have thoroughly taught him, he would have needed to take Bill 'bush'; that is, somewhere where there is solitude and that his training would have required something in the order of eight years. Namadbara makes this meaning clear further on in Bill's account.
54 See Pizzy (1980:109) for description of the call, the night-time 'wail of the curlew'.
55 I am using 'a meditative state' in the particular sense of a mental state in which there is conscious awareness without thought arising commenting on that awareness. The text supports the interpretation that Namadbara is talking about a deliberate cultivation of this state as a pre-condition for communication with, for instance, 'the tree' and for accessing marrngkidj, the power.
56 What is remarkable about Bill's rendition is that it clearly preserves the instructions and the integrity of a powerful philosophy or practice, even though he himself had not yet been able to carry it through or to master the practice.
57 See Coate's (1966–7:102–103) translation of Mowarldjarlai's text: 'Then he opened a tree for him . . . the *rai* . . . opens a tree for the novice [magician] . . . this is what you do to open a tree; fire at it with magic stones . . . In case a man should chase you, that's how you do', and also Elkin (1977:54): 'Another [clever man] hit a tree and disappeared into it, like a stone sinking into muddy water'.
58 See earlier account of this occurrence in the section on Namadbara's 'power objects' and compare Bates (1985) — refer to endnote 48.
59 The variety of antbed (i.e. termite mound), in this case said to be black. Compare Garde (2020).
60 Locations where this power is inherent are called 'poison' sites; only three occur in Western Arnhem Land. Namadbara had control over one of these, a major kundjak site on his Country, located at Lanka (Mt Permain). The 'poison' can be wielded and is capable of killing people. Namadbara was the only one with the authority to go there and, even into the late 1990s, it was said that there was no one with the necessary qualifications to visit the place. See O'Connor (2011); Lamilami (1974); Berndt (1970).
61 I use the term 'spirit' but acknowledge its lack of precision and my own lack of knowledge of what it might refer to.
62 In writing of post-death understandings of the Northern Territory Port Keats–Daly people, Marett (2000:24–25) refers to a person's conception spirit (maruy) at death, which ceases to be human and becomes a ghost — a wunymalang. 'Wunymalang who have been properly conducted away from human society . . . live in the bush . . . in the country where people continue to hunt and forage. They have the capacity to "come out" from the country when they sense the presence of relatives (whom they look after) or strangers (from whom they will protect relatives). They will also appear to people in dreams and can be called up by ritual calling or singing.'
63 Interestingly, anthropologist Brian Morris (2006:23), in speaking of shamanism in general, maintained 'that the most famous shaman or spirit-medium in history was, of course, Jesus of Nazareth, although many Christians and some anthropologists seem to

64 It is interesting to note in regard to both Namadbara and Wilambilam's influence in Gunbalanya, Berndt (1964:274) considered that it would have been even greater if they had been traditional owners of that Country (i.e. through traditional patrilineal inheritance of the land there) and had had the consequent additional ceremonial authority.
65 Pers. comm. 1991.
66 In recent work, physicists Stephen Hawking and Leonard Mlodinow spoke of reality as being completely 'model dependent' (Hawking & Mlodinow 2010). In Hawking's final paper in 2018 with physicist Thomas Hertog, he postulates that the universe is in fact 'a large and complex hologram' (Hertog 2018). Some have long proposed that the model of such a holographic universe provides the basis for understanding a host of clever phenomena (see Talbot 2011; Mitchell & Staretz 2011). Anthropologist Margaret Mead was considered radical in the 1970s in her belief that scientific understanding would eventually accommodate these phenomena and observed that 'we are living on the edge of the unknown in terms of . . . greatly expanded knowledge of our human sensibilities and capacities' (quoted in Lett 1991:307).
67 Compare the West Arnhem synonymous term 'kunmalng' — life force, spirit, vital energy.
68 I am referring specifically to how the matter of 'clever men' has been dealt with in the literature. Of course there are exceptions, e.g. Berndt (1947).
69 Elkin (1977:65) considered that: 'We have found the external universe of overwhelming interest and sought . . . its explanations in mechanical and physical laws. We have endeavoured . . . to apply those same laws to man as an individual and social being . . . It is possible that this approach has led to our neglecting, or to considering as unworthy or unscientific, certain phenomena which men have claimed to be important and potent . . . But it is scientific to study all phenomena, and to do so patiently, objectively and, if necessary, with new approaches. And the powers of the human mind are worthy of such investigation. We of the West are so intellectual, so rational . . . that we have inhibited real freedom of thought [in this regard]'.
70 This 'shift' has now developed into a distinct scientific uncertainty as to the nature of reality. It is a prominent feature of debates and discussions among physicists, cosmologists, and philosophers. A recent New Scientist cover story 'What is Reality? The more we look at it the less real it becomes' sums up the situation: 'We are now at the point where it is equally credible to claim that reality is entirely dependent on subjective experience, or entirely independent of it. Reality never felt so unreal.' (New Scientist, 1 February 2020:34)
71 Samuel (1993:8) writes: 'I use the term "shamanic" as a general term for a category of practices found in differing degrees in almost all human societies . . . [this may be described as] the regulation and transformation of human life and human society through the use (or purported use) of alternate states of consciousness by which specialist practitioners are held to communicate with a mode of reality alternative to, or more fundamental than, the world of everyday experience.' Also, see Winkelman (2010:59–61) for discussion regarding the use of the term.
72 Physicist Adam Frank (2017:np) writes: Materialists appeal to physics to explain the mind, but in modern physics the particles that make up the brain remain, in many ways, as mysterious as consciousness itself . . . after more than a century of profound explorations into the sub-atomic world, our best theory for *how matter behaves* still tells us very little about *what matter is*. In the very public version of the debate over consciousness, those who advocate that understanding the mind might require something other than a 'nothing but matter' position are often painted as victims of wishful thinking, imprecise reasoning or, worst of all, an adherence to a mystical 'woo' [his emphasis].
73 The 'subtle body' is a generic term covering a variety of Asian yogic and tantric practices involving healings and mind-body transformations — including such concepts as the Chinese chi/qi channels or 'meridians', the Indian yogic chakras and prana, Tibetan 'special dream-bodies', and similar concepts within Sufism (e.g. Corbin 1972), all conceived as occupying an interstitial position between body and mind. Interestingly, they have much in common with some Aboriginal understandings and practices — for instance, the South Australian Yaraldi claims of the powers that come with the development of the miwi (Berndt et. al 1993) compare compellingly with the powers that come with the development of 'chi' (see Liao 2009; Wong 2007; Swartz 1994:233–235; Samuel & Johnston 2013).

Bibliography

Abram, D. 1997. *The Spell of the Sensuous: Perception and Language in a More-Than-Human World*. New York: Vintage.
Abram, D. 2010. *Becoming Animal: An Earthly Cosmology*. New York: Pantheon.
Abram, D. 2013. The invisibles: Towards a phenomenology of the spirits. In *The Handbook of Contemporary Animism*, (ed.) G. Harvey, pp. 124–132. Durham: Acumen.
Akerman, K. 1979. Contemporary Aboriginal healers in the South Kimberley. *Oceania* 50(1):23–30.
Angoff, A. and D. Barth (eds). 1974. Parapsychology and Anthropology. Proceedings of an international conference held in London, England, August 29–31, 1973. New York: Parapsychology Foundation.
Atkinson, J. M. 1992. Shamanisms today. *Annual Review of Anthropology* 21:307–33.
Barad, K. 2007. *Meeting The Universe Halfway: Quantum physics and the entanglement of matter and meaning*. Durham: Duke University Press.
Bates, D. 1985. *The Native Tribes of Western Australia*, (ed.) I. White. Canberra: National Library of Australia.
Beals, R.L. 1978. Sonoran fantasy or coming of age? *American Anthropologist* 80:355–362.
Becker, A. 2018. *What is Real?: The Unfinished Quest for the Meaning of Quantum Physics*. New York: Basis Books.
Beckett, J. 1977. Preface. In *Aboriginal Men of High Degree* (2nd edn.) A.P. Elkin. Pp. ix–xv. St. Lucia: University of Queensland Press.
Berndt, C.H. 1964. The role of native doctors in Aboriginal Australia. In *Magic, Faith, and Healing: Studies in primitive psychiatry today*, (ed.) A. Kiev, pp. 264–282. New York: The Free Press of Glencoe.
Berndt, C.H. 1984. Sickness and Health in Western Arnhem land: A traditional perspective. In *Body, Land and Spirit: Health and Healing in Aboriginal Society*, (ed.) J. Reid, pp. 121–138. St. Lucia: University of Queensland Press.
Berndt, R.M. 1947. Wiradjuri magic and 'clever men'. *Oceania* 17(4):327– 365; 18(1):60–86.
Berndt, R.M. 1970. *The Sacred Site: The Western Arnhem Land Example*. Canberra: Australian Institute of Aboriginal Studies.
Berndt, R.M. 1979. A Profile of Good and Bad in Australian Aboriginal Religion. Charles Strong (Australian Church) Memorial Trust. Reprinted from *Colloquium Journal* of the ANZSTS, Melbourne.
Berndt, R.M. & C.H. Berndt. 1951. The concept of abnormality in an Australian Aboriginal society. In *Psychoanalysis and Culture: Essays in honour of Geza Roheim*, (eds) G.B. Wilbur and W. Muensterberger, pp. 75–89. New York: International Universities Press.
Berndt, R.M. & C.H. Berndt. 1970. *Man, Land, and Myth in North Australia: The Gunwinggu people*. Sydney: Ure Smith.
Berndt, R.M. & C.H. Berndt. 1988. *The Speaking Land*. Ringwood: Penguin.
Berndt, R.M. & C.H. Berndt. 1992. *The World of the First Australians*. (5th edn). Canberra: Australian Studies Press.
Berndt R.M., C.H. Berndt, and J.E. Stanton. 1982. *Aboriginal Australian Art: A Visual Perspective*. Sydney: Methuen.
Berndt R.M. & C.H. Berndt, with J.E. Stanton. 1993. *A World That Was: The Yaraldi of the Murray River and the Lakes, South Australia*. Carlton: Melbourne University Press.

Birch, B. 2011. The American Clever Man (Marrkijbu Burdan Merika). In *Exploring the Legacy of the 1948 Arnhem Land Expedition*, (eds) Martin Thomas and M. Neale, pp. 313–336. Canberra: Australian National University Press.
Blackmore, S. 2012. *Consciousness: An Introduction* (2nd edn). New York: Oxford University Press.
Bourguignon, E. (ed.). 1973. *Religion, Altered States of Consciousness, and Social Change*. Columbus: Ohio State University Press.
Bowie, Fiona. [n.d.] Believing Impossible Things: Scepticism and Ethnographic Enquiry. Typescript 32 pages. From Fiona Bowie's entry on Academia.com website (accessed 28/04/2017).
Butala, S. 2005 [1994]. *The Perfection of the Morning: An Apprenticeship in Nature*. Toronto: Harper Perennial Canada.
Cane, S. 2002. *Pila Nguru: The Spinifex People*. Fremantle: Fremantle Arts Press.
Caruana, W. 1993. *Aboriginal Art*. London: Thames & Hudson.
Cawte, J. 1964. Tjimi and tjagolo: Ethnopsychiatry in the Kalumburu people of north-western Australia. *Oceania* 34(3):170–190.
Cawte, J. 1974. *Medicine is the Law: Studies in Psychiatric Anthropology of Australian tribes*. Adelaide: Rigby (University of Hawaii Press).
Chalmers, D. 1995. Facing up to the problem of consciousness. *Journal of Consciousness Studies* 3:200–219.
Chaloupka, G. 1993. *Journey in Time: The World's Longest Continuing Art Tradition*. Chatswood: Reed.
Chaloupka, G., N. Kapirigi, B. Nayidji & G. Namingum. 1985. Cultural Survey of Balawurru, Deaf Adder Creek; Amarrkananga, Cannon Hill and the Northern Corridor. A report to the Australian National Parks and Wildlife Service. Darwin: Australian National Parks and Wildlife Service and The Museum and Art Galleries Board of the Northern Territory. [typescript].
Charlesworth, M. 1984. Introduction. In *Religion in Aboriginal Australia: An Anthology*, (eds) M. Charlesworth, H. Morphy, D. Bell, and K. Maddock, pp. 1–20. St Lucia: University of Queensland Press.
Chaudhuri, H. 2002. Yogic Potentials and Capacities (Siddhis). *Esalen Centre for Theory and Research*. Available at http://www.esalen.org/ctr-archive/yogic_capacities.html (accessed 11/08/2014).
Clarke, P. 2008. Aboriginal healing practices and Australian bush medicine. *Journal of the Anthropological Society of South Australia* 33:3–38.
Coate, H.H.J. 1966–7. The rai and the third eye: north-west Australian beliefs. *Oceania* 37:93–123.
Cole, K. 1975. *A History of Oenpelli*. Darwin: Nungalinya Publications.
Cole, K. 1979. *The Aborigines of Arnhem Land*. Adelaide: Rigby.
Colorado, P. 1992. Wayfaring and the New Sun: Indigenous Science in the Modern World. *Noetic Sciences Review Summer* pp. 19–23.
Corbin, H. 1972. Mundus Imaginalis Or the Imaginary and the Imaginal. *Spring*: pp. 1–19.
Corbin, H. 1997 [1969]. *Alone with the Alone: Creative Imagination in the Sufism of Ibn 'Arabi*. Princeton. New Jersey: Bollingen Series XCI Princeton University Press.
Crick, M. R. 1982 Anthropology of knowledge. *Annual Review of Anthropology* 11:287–313.
De Mille, R. 1976. *Castaneda's Journey: The Power and the Allegory*. Santa Barbara: Capra Press.
De Mille, R. (ed.) 1980. *The Don Juan Papers: Further Castaneda Controversies*. Santa Barbara: Ross-Erikson.
Dobkin de Rios, M. 1982. 'CA Comment' on M. Winkelman 'Magic: A Theoretical Reassessment'. *Current Anthropology* 23(1):37–66.
Eastwell, H.D. 1973. The traditional healer in modern Arnhem Land. *The Medical Journal of Australia* 2:1011–1017.

Eastwell, H.D. 1982a. Australian Aboriginal Mental Health — Overview. *Transcultural Psychiatric Research Review* 19:221–247.
Eastwell, H.D. 1982b. Voodoo death and the mechanism for dispatch of the dying in East Arnhem, Australia. *American Anthropologist* 84: 5–18.
Edwards, G. 1973. Ancient burial site reveals its secrets. *Northern Territory Affairs*, vol. 7, May 1973: 3–5.
Eliade, M. 1964 [1951]. *Shamanism: Archaic techniques of ecstasy.* [Trans. W.R. Trask]. Bollingen: Princeton University Press.
Eliade, M. 1968. Myths, Dreams & Mysteries. London: Collins.
Eliade, M. 1987. Shamanism and cosmology. In Shamanism: An Expanded View of Reality. S. Nicholson ed. Pp. 17–46. Wheaton, Ill.: Theosophical Publishing House.
Elkin, A.P. 1977 [1945]. *Aboriginal Men of High Degree*. (2nd edn) St Lucia, Queensland: University of Queensland Press.
Evans, N. 1991. Study and production of an orthography for the Gun-djeipmi language, Alligator Rivers Region, Phase II. A consultancy report prepared for the Australian National Parks & Wildlife Service. Part I: Mayali Texts; Part II: How to write Gundjeihmi; Part III: Mayali Dictionary. ANPWS: Kakadu National Park.
Evans, N. 2018. *Words of Life*. Essay, The Clearing, Little Toller Books. Available at https://www.littletoller.co.uk/the-clearing/poetry/words-of-life-by-nicholas-evans/ (accessed 20/05/2019).
Frank, A. 2017. Minding Matter. *Aeon – online magazine*, 13 March. Available at https://aeon.co/essays/materialism-alone-cannot-explain-the-riddle-of-consciousness (accessed 19/03/2017).
Fuchs, C. 2015. 'Quantum worlds.' ABC Radio National 'The Philosopher's Stone'. Available at www.abc.net.au/radionational/programs/philosopherszone/fuchs/6774368 (accessed 06/02/2020).
Garde, M. 2013. *Culture, Interaction and Personal Reference in an Australian Language*. Amsterdam: John Benjamins.
Garde, M. 2020. Bininj Kunwok dictionary. Available at https://www.njamed.com (accessed 06/02/2020).
Glaskin, K. 2008. Dreams and memory: accessing metaphysical realms in the northwest Kimberley. *Journal of the Anthropological Society of South Australia* 33:39–73.
Glass-Coffin, Bonnie. 2010. Anthropology, Shamanism, and Alternate Ways of Knowing-Being in the World: One Anthropologist's Journey of Discovery and Transformation. *Anthropology and Humanism* 35(2):204–217.
Greenwood, S. 2000. *Magic, Witchcraft and the Otherworld: An Anthropology*. Oxford: Berg.
Greenwood, S. 2006. *The Nature of Magic: An Anthropology of Consciousness*. Oxford: Berg.
Greenwood, S. 2009. *The Anthropology of Magic*. Oxford: Berg.
Harner, M. 1982. *The Way of the Shaman*. Toronto: Bantam.
Harner, M. 2013. *Cave and Cosmos: Shamanic Encounters with Another Reality*. Berkeley, CA: North Atlantic Books.
Harvey, G. 2006. *Animism: Respecting the Living World*. New York: Columbia University Press.
Hawking, S. and L. Mlodinow. 2010. *The Grand Design*. New York: Bantam.
Haydon, T. 1974. *Long, Long Walkabout*. Motion picture. BBC-TV with Australian Broadcasting Commission.
Heinze, Ruth-Inge. 1993. Shamanic states of consciousness: access to different realities. In *Shamans and Cultures*, (eds) M. Hoppal and K.D. Howard, pp. 169–178. Budapest: Akademiai Kaido/Los Angeles: International Society for Trans-Oceanic Research.
Hertog, T. 2018. Hawking's last paper co-authored with ERC grantee posits new cosmology. Interview with ERC grantee Thomas Hertog. Available at https://www.curekalert.org/pub_releases/2018-05/

erc-hlp043018.php (accessed 31/03/2019).
Hess, D.J. 1993. *Science in the New Age: The Paranormal, its Defenders and Debunkers, and American Culture*. Madison, Wisconsin: University of Wisconsin.
Hill, E. 1951. *The Territory*. Sydney: Angus & Robertson.
Hoeng, S. n.d. Continuity and change in the artistic system of north-western Arnhem Land. Form and meaning in paintings from the 1870s to the 1980s. Uncompleted PhD research. Australian National University, School of Archaeology and Anthropology, Canberra.
Hoppal, M. 1993. Shamanism: universal structures and regional symbols. In *Shamans and Cultures*, (eds) M. Hoppal and K.D. Howard, pp. 181–192. Budapest: Akademiai Kaido/Los Angeles: International Society for Trans-Oceanic Research.
Hoppal, M. and K.D. Howard (eds). 1993. *Shamans and Cultures*. Budapest: Akademiai Kaido/Los Angeles: International Society for Trans-Oceanic Research.
Howell, Julia. 1989. The Social Sciences and Mystical Experience. In *Exploring the Paranormal: Perspectives on Belief and Experience*, (eds) G.K. Zollschan, J.F. Schumaker, and G.F. Walsh, pp. 77–94. Bridport, Dorset: Prism.
Hultkrantz, A. 1988. Shamanism: A religious phenomenon? In *Shaman's Path*, (ed.) G. Doore, pp. 33–41. Boston: Shambala.
Hume, L. 1997. *Witchcraft and Paganism in Australia*. Carlton: Melbourne University Press.
Hume, L. 2002. *Ancestral Power: The Dreaming, Consciousness and Aboriginal Australians*. Carlton: Melbourne University Press.
Hume, L. 2007. Portals: Opening Doorways to Other Realities through the Senses. Oxford: Berg.
Jacobsen, K. 2012. Introduction: Yoga powers and religious traditions. In *Yoga Powers: Extraordinary Capacities Attained Through Meditation and Concentration*, (ed.) Knut Jacobsen, pp. 1–31. Leiden: Brill. Available at https://www.scribd.com/document/339262839/Jacobsen-Knut-a-Yoga-Powers-Extraordinary-Cap-Bookzz-org (accessed 6/4/2017).
Kahn, J.S. 2014. Encountering extraordinary worlds: The rules of ethnographic engagement and the limits of anthropological knowing. *Numen* 61:237–254.
Kaiser, D. 2012. *How the Hippies Saved Physics*. New York: Norton.
Kapferer, B. 2003. Introduction: Outside all reason: Magic, sorcery and epistemology in anthropology. In *Beyond Rationalism: Rethinking Magic, Witchcraft and Sorcery*, (ed.) B. Kapferer, pp. 1–30. New York: Berghahn Books.
Katz, R. 1982. *Boiling Energy: Community Healing among the Kalahari Kung*. Cambridge, MA: Harvard University Press.
Katz, R. 1989. Healing and transformation: Perspectives from !Kung hunter-gatherers. In *Altered States of Consciousness and Mental Health: A Cross-cultural Perspective*, (ed.) C.A. Ward, pp. 207–222. Newbury Park: Sage.
Kelly, E.F. and I. Whicher. 2015. Patanjali's yoga sutras and the siddhis. In *Beyond Physicalism*, (eds) E.F. Kelly, A. Crabtree and P. Marshall, pp. 315–348. Lanham, MD: Rowman & Littlefield.
Kripal, J. 2012. The evolving siddhis: Yoga and tantra in the human-potential movement and beyond. In *Yoga Powers: Extraordinary Capacities Attained Through Meditation and Concentration*, (ed.) Knut Jacobsen, pp. 479–508. Leiden: Brill.
Kupka, K. 1972. *Peintres Aborigines d'Australie*. Paris: Societie des Oceanistes.
Laderman, C. 1993. *Taming the Wind of Desire: Psychology, Medicine and Aesthetics in Malay Shamanistic Performance*. Berkeley: University of California.
Lamilami, Rev. L. 1974. *Lamilami Speaks: The Cry Went Up: A Story of the People of Goulburn Islands, North Australia*. Sydney: Ure Smith.
Laughlin, C.D. 1994. Psychic energy and transpersonal experience: A biogenetic structural account of

Tibetan dumo yoga practice. In *Being Changed by Cross-Cultural Encounters: The Anthropology of Extraordinary Experience*, (eds) D.A. Young and G-J. Goulet, pp. 99–134. Ontario: Broadview Press.

Lett, J. 1991. Interpretive anthropology, metaphysics, and the paranormal. *Journal of Anthropological Research* 47(3):305–329.

Levitus, R. 1995. Social history since colonization. In *Kakadu: Natural and Cultural Heritage and Management*, (eds) T. Press, D. Lea, A. Webb and A. Graham, pp. 64–93. Darwin: Australian Nature Conservation Agency/North Australia Research Unit/Australian National University.

Liao, Waysun. 2009. *Chi: Discovering Your Life Energy*. Boston: Shambala.

Linde, A. 1998. Universe, Life, Consciousness. Paper delivered at the Physics and Cosmology Group of the 'Science and Spirituality Quest' program of the Center for Theology and Natural Sciences, Berkeley, CA. Available at web.stanford.edu/~alinde/SpirQuest.doc (accessed 07/04/2018).

Lockwood, D. 1962. *I, the Aboriginal*. Adelaide: Rigby.

Lommel, A. and D. Mowaljalai. 1994. Shamanism in northwest Australia. *Oceania* 64(4):277–287.

Luke, David 2010. Anthropology and parapsychology: Still hostile sisters in science? *Time and Mind: The Journal of Archaeology, Consciousness and Culture* 3(3):245–266. Available at http://dx.doi10.2752/17569610X12754030955850

McCaul, K. 2008. The persistence of traditional healers in the 21st century and of anthropology's struggle to understand them. *Journal of the Anthropological Society of South Australia* 33:129–166.

McCaul, K. 2016. The making of a Simpson Desert clever man. In *Language, Land and Song*, (eds) Peter K. Austin, Harold Koch and Jane Simpson, pp. 344–357. London: EL Publishing.

McCoy, Brian F. 2008. Outside the ward and clinic: Healing the Aboriginal body. *Journal of Contemporary Ethnography* 37(2): 226–245.

Macknight, C.C. 1976. *The Voyage to Marege: Macassan Trepangers in Northern Australia*. Melbourne: Melbourne University Press.

McIntosh, I. 1994. *The Whale and the Cross: Conversations with David Burrumarra MBE*. Darwin: Historical Society of the Northern Territory.

McClenon, J. 1993. The experiential foundation of shamanic healing. *Journal of Medicine & Philosophy* 18(2):107–128.

Marett, A. 2000. Ghostly voices: some observations on song creation, ceremony and being in north-west Australia. *Oceania* 71(1):18–29

Marett, A. 2009. *Songs, Dreamings, and Ghosts: The Wangga of North Australia*. Middletown, CONN: Wesleyan University Press.

Mayer, Elizabeth, L. 2008. *Extraordinary Knowing: Science, Skepticism, and the Inexplicable Powers of the Human Mind*. New York: Bantam Books.

Mensky, Michael, B. 2011. Logic of quantum mechanics and phenomenon of consciousness. In *Quantum Physics of Consciousness: Selections from Volumes 3 and 14 Journal of Cosmology*, (eds) S. Kak, R. Penrose and S. Hameroff, pp. 133–145. Cambridge, MA: Cosmology Science Publishers.

Musser, G. 2015. *Spooky Action at a Distance: The Phenomenon that Reimagines Space and Time–And What it Means for Black Holes, the Big Bang, and Theories of Everything*. New York: Scientific American/Farrar, Straus and Giroux.

Mitchell, Edgar and R. Staretz. 2011. The quantum hologram and the nature of consciousness. In *Quantum Physics of Consciousness: Selections from Volumes 3 and 14 Journal of Cosmology*. (eds) S. Kak, R. Penrose and S. Hameroff, pp. 190–222. Cambridge MA: Cosmology Science Publishers.

Morphy, H. 1988. The resurrection of the Hydra: twenty-five years of research on Aboriginal religion. In *Social Anthropology and Australian Aboriginal Studies: A Contemporary Overview*, (eds) R. M. Berndt and R. Tonkinson, pp. 241–266. Canberra: Aboriginal Studies Press.

Morris, B. 2006. *Religion and Anthropology: A Critical Introduction*. Cambridge: Cambridge University Press.
Mowaljarlai, D. and J. Malnic. 1993. *Yorro Yorro. Everything standing up alive: Spirit of the Kimberley*. Broome: Magabala.
Mulvaney, J.D. and J. H. Calaby. 1985. *So Much that is New: Baldwin Spencer, 1860–1929*. Carlton: Melbourne University Press.
Murphy, J. 1964. Psychotherapeutic aspects of shamanism on St. Lawrence Island, Alaska. In *Magic, Faith and Healing: Studies in Primitive Psychiatry Today*, (ed.) A. Kiev, pp. 53–83. New York: The Free Press.
Nadasdy, P. 2007. The gift in the animal: The ontology of hunting and human-animal sociality. *American Ethnologist* 34(1):25–43.
Neidjie, B. 1989. *Story about Feeling*. Broome: Magabala Books.
Neidjie, B.B., S. Davis and A. Fox. 1986. *Australia's Kakadu Man Bill Neidjie*. Darwin: Resource Managers Pty Ltd.
Nelson, Peter L. and Julia D. Howell. 1993–4. A psycho-social phenomenological methodology for conducting operational, ontologically neutral research into religious and altered state experiences. *Journal for the Psychology of Religion* 2–3:1–48.
Noll, R. 1985 Mental imagery cultivation as a cultural phenomenon: The role of visions in shamanism. *Current Anthropology* 26(4):443–461.
Ngaanyatjarra Pitjantjatjara Yankunytjatjara (NPY) Women's Council Aboriginal Corporation. 2013. *Traditional Healers of Central Australia: Ngangkari*. Broome: Magabala Books.
Obeyesekere, G. 2012. *The Awakened Ones: Phenomenology of Visionary Experience*. New York: Columbia University Press.
O'Connor, P. 2011. *Lunga Hill of Death: Eight True Life Stories – Drawn from Personal Experiences of Living in Arnhem Land*. Self-published: Buderim, Queensland.
O'Ferrall, M. 1990. *Keepers of the Secrets: Aboriginal Art from Arnhem Land*. Perth: Art Gallery of Western Australia.
Petri, H. 2014. *The Australian Medicine Man*. (English translation of *Der Austalische Medizenmann*, 1952, trans. Ian Campbell), (ed.) Kim Akerman,. Victoria Park, WA: Hesperian Press.
Pizzy, G. 1980. *A Field Guide to the Birds of Australia*. Sydney: Collins.
Poirier, S. 2016. The dynamic reproduction of hunter-gatherers' ontologies and values. In *A Companion to the Anthropology of Religion*, (eds) J. Boddy and M. Lambek, pp. 50–68. Chichester: Wiley/Blackwell.
Pollan, M. 2018. *How To change Your Mind: The New Science of Psychedelics*. Allen Lane.
Price-Williams, D. 1987. The waking dream in ethnographic perspective. In *Dreaming: anthropological and psychological interpretations*, (ed.) B. Tedlock, pp. 246–262. Cambridge: Cambridge University Press.
Radin, D. 2013. *Supernormal: Science, Yoga, and the Evidence for Extraordinary Psychic Abilities*. New York: Deepak Chopra Books/Random House.
Read, P. 2003. *Haunted Earth*. Sydney: University of New South Wales Press.
Reanney, D. 1994. *Music of the Mind: An Adventure into Consciousness*. Melbourne: Hill of Content.
Reid, J. 1980. Sorcery and healing: The meaning of illness and death to an Australian Aboriginal community. PhD thesis, Stanford University, 1978. Ann Arbor: University Microfilms.
Reid, J. 1983. *Sorcerers and Healing Spirits: Continuity and Change in an Aboriginal Medical System*. Rushcutter's Bay, NSW: Pergamon.
Reid, J. (ed.) 1984 *Body, Land and Spirit: Health and Healing in Aboriginal Society*. St. Lucia: University of Queensland Press.

Rocha, C. 2017. *John of God: The Globalization of Brazilian Faith Healing*. Oxford: Oxford University Press.

Rodd, R. 2011. Metaphysical beliefs associated with Ayahuasca experiences and consciousness research. Paper delivered at Australian Anthropological Society Conference, University of Western Australia, Perth [typescript]. Available at http://www.anthropologywa.org/iuaes_aas_asaanz_conference2011/0066.ht#s1p1 (accessed 23/07/2017).

Rosenblum, B. and F. Kuttner. 2011. *Quantum Enigma: Physics Encounters Consciousness*. (2nd edn.) New York: Oxford University Press.

Roth, W. E. 1984 [1903]. *The Queensland Aborigines*. Carslile, WA: Hesperian. [Fasc. ed. 1903 *North Queensland Ethnography*: Bulletin No. 5. Superstition, Magic, and Medicine.]

Rothwell, Nicolas. 2003. That Old Black Magic: The healing hand of a Western Desert medicine man, Jacky Giles, touches Nicolas Rothwell. He emerges a changed man. *Weekend Australian Magazine*, May 17–18, pp. 24–27.

Sales, K. 1992. Ascent to the sky. A shamanic initiatory engraving from the Burrup Peninsula, northwest Western Australia. *Archaeology in Oceania* 27(1):22–35.

Samuel, G. 1990. *Mind, Body, and Culture: Anthropology and the Biological Interface*. Cambridge: Cambridge University Press.

Samuel, G. 1993. *Civilised Shamans: Buddhism in Tibetan societies*. Washington, DC: Smithsonian Institution Press.

Samuel, G. 2013. Subtle-body processes: towards a non-reductionist understanding. In *Religion and the Subtle Body in Asia and the West*, (eds) G. Samuel and Jay Johnston, pp. 249–266. London: Routledge.

Samuel, G. and J. Johnston. 2013 (eds). *Religion and the Subtle Body in Asia and the West*. London: Routledge.

San Roque, C. 2011. Sigmund Freud Award Speech: Philosophy of the Ngangkari. Available from https://www.npywc.org.au/sigmund-freud-award-speech/ (accessed 23/08/2017).

Searcy, A. 1984 [1909]. *In Australian Tropics*. Victoria Park, WA: Hesperian.

Sered, Susan. 2003. Afterword: Lexicons of the supernatural. *Anthropological Forum* 13(2):213–218.

Shirokogoroff, S.M. 1999 [1935]. *The Psychomental Complex of the Tungus*. Berlin: Reinhold Schletzer Verlag.

Siskin, E. 1983. *Washo Shamans and Peyotists: Religious Conflict in an American Indian Tribe*. Salt Lake City: University of Utah Press.

Snaprud, P. 2018. Consciousness: How we're solving a mystery bigger than our minds. *New Scientist*. Available at https://www.newscientist.com/article/mg23831830-300-consciousness-how-were-solving-a-mystery-bigger-than-our-minds/ (accessed 22/06/2018).

Spencer, W.B. 1914. Native Tribes of the Northern Territory of Australia. London: Macmillan.

Stapp, H. P. 2007a. *Mindful Universe: Quantum Mechanics and the Participating Observer*. Berlin: Springer Verlag.

Stapp, H. P. 2007b. Quantum mechanical theories of consciousness. In *The Blackwell Companion to Consciousness*, (eds) Max Velmans and Susan Schneider, pp. 300–312. Blackwell Publishing: Malden, MA. Available at www-physics.lbl.gov/~stapp/stappfiles.html (accessed 15/04/2016).

St John, G. 2015. *Mystery School in Hyperspace: A Cultural History of DMT*. Berkeley: North Atlantic Books.

Stephen, M. 1979. Dreams of change: The innovative role of altered states of consciousness in traditional Melanesian religion. *Oceania* 50(1):3–22.

Stephen, M. 1995. *A'aisa's Gifts: A Study of Magic and the Self*. Berkeley: University of California Press.

Stephen, M. 1996. The Mekeo 'man of sorrow': Sorcery and the individuation of the self. *American*

Ethnologist 23(1):83–101.
Stoller, P. and C. Olkes. 1987. *In Sorcery's Shadow: A Memoir of Apprenticeship among the Songhay of Niger*. Chicago: University of Chicago Press.
Stoller, P. 1989. *The Taste of Ethnographic Things: The Senses in Anthropology*. Philadelphia: University of Pennsylvania Press.
Sumegi, A. 2013. On souls and subtle bodies: a comparison of shamanic and Buddhist perspectives. In *Religion and the Subtle Body in Asia and the West*, (eds) G. Samuel and Jay Johnston, pp. 69–82. London: Routledge.
Swartz, L. 1994. Being changed by cross-cultural encounters. In *Being Changed by Cross-Cultural Encounters: The Anthropology of Extraordinary Experience*, (eds) D.E. Young and Jean-Guy Goulet, pp. 209–236. Ontario: Broadview Press.
Talbot, M. 2011 [1991]. *The Holographic Universe*. New York: Harper Perennial.
Tambiah, S. J. 1990. *Magic, Science, Religion and the Scope of Rationality*. Cambridge: Cambridge University Press.
Tarnas, R. 1991. *The Passion of the Western Mind: Understanding the Ideas That Have Shaped Our World View*. New York: Ballantine Books.
Tart, C.T. (ed.) 1972. *Altered States of Consciousness*. New York: Doubleday Anchor Books.
Tart, C.T. 1980. A systems approach to altered states of consciousness. In *The Psychobiology of Consciousness*, (eds) J.M. and R.J. Davidson, pp. 243–269. New York: Plenum.
Tart, C.T. 1998. Investigating altered states of consciousness on their own terms: A proposal for the creation of state-specific sciences. *Journal of the Brazilian Association for the Advancement of Science* (50):103– 116. Available at http://www.paradigm-sys.com/ctt_article2.cfm?id=42 (accessed 27/07/2011).
Taylor, L. 1987. 'The same but different': Social reproduction and innovation in the art of the Kunwinjku of Western Arnhem Land. PhD thesis, Australian National University, Canberra.
Thompson, E. 2015. *Waking, Dreaming, Being: Self and Consciousness in Neuroscience, Meditation, and Philosophy*. New York: Columbia University Press.
Tonkinson, M. 1984. The mabarn and the hospital: the selection of treatment in a remote Aboriginal community. In *Body, Land and Spirit*, (ed.) J. Reid, pp. 225–241. St. Lucia: University of Queensland Press.
Tonkinson, R. 1978. *The Mardudjara Aborigines: Living the Dream in Australia's Desert*. New York: Holt, Reinhart and Winston.
Tonkinson, R. 1991. *The Mardu Aborigines: Living the Dream in Australia's Desert*. (2nd edn.). Fort Worth: Holt, Reinhart and Winston.
Tonkinson, R. 1993. Foreword. In *A World That Was: The Yaraldi of the Murray River and the Lakes, South Australia*, R.M. Berndt and C.H. Berndt, with J.E. Stanton, pp. xvii–xxxi. Carlton: Melbourne University Press.
Turner, E. 1993. The reality of spirits: A tabooed or permitted field of study? *Anthropology of Consciousness* 4(1):9–12.
Varela F. J. (ed.) 1997. *Sleeping, Dreaming, and Dying: An Exploration of Consciousness with the Dalai Lama*. Boston: Wisdom Publications.
Varela, F. J., E. Thompson and E. Rosch. 1991. *The Embodied Mind: Cognitive Science and Human Experience*. Cambridge, Massachusetts: The MIT Press.
Varela, F. J. and J. Shear (eds) 1999. *The View from Within: First-person Approaches to the Study of Consciousness*. Thorverton: Imprint Academic.
Wallace, B. Alan. 1999. The Buddhist tradition of Samatha: Methods for refining and examining consciousness. In *The View from Within: First-person Approaches to the Study of Consciousness*,

(eds) J. Varela and J. Shear, pp. 175–187. Thorverton: Imprint Academic.
Wallace, B. Alan. 2000. *The Taboo of Subjectivity: Toward a New Science of Consciousness*. Oxford: Oxford University Press.
Whimpress, B. and I. Cooper. 2018. *Buffalo Men*. Published by Ian Cooper: tarisa@chariot.com.au
White, I. and J. Nayinggul. 2002. Nurturing the sacred in western Arnhem Land. *Cultural Survival Quarterly* 26(2):15–17.
Winkelman, M. 2010. *Shamanism: A Biopsychosocial Paradigm of Consciousness and Healing*. (2nd edn). Santa Barbara: Praeger.
Wise, T. 1985. *The Self-Made Anthropologist: A life of A.P. Elkin*. Sydney: George Allen and Unwin.
Wong, Kiew Kit, 2007. *Chi Kung for Health and Vitality: A Practical Approach to the Art of Energy*. Cosmos Press. Availabe at www.cosmospress.com
Young, D. E. and Jean-Guy Goulet (eds). 1994. *Being Changed by Cross-Cultural Encounters: The Anthropology of Extraordinary Experience*. Ontario: Broadview Press.